SWU-800- 001

UNIFORMS OF RUSSIAN ARMY DURING THE YEARS 1825-1855 VOL. 1

UNDER THE REIGN OF NICHOLAS I
EMPEROR OF RUSSIA BETWEEN 1825 TO 1855
GRENADIER AND INFANTRY

From the Viskovatov's greatest work:
"Historical description of the clothing and
arms of the Russian Army"

English translation by Mark Conrad

SOLDIERSHOP PUBLISHING

AUTHOR

Aleksandr Vasilevich Viskovatov born 22 April (4 May New Style) 1804, died 27 February (11 March) 1858 in St. Petersburg, Russian military historian. He graduated from the 1st Cadet Corps and served in the artillery, the hydrographic depot of the Naval Ministry, and then in the Department of Military Educational Institutions. He mainly studied historical artifacts and the histories of military units. Viskovatov's greatest work was the Historical Description of the Clothing and Arms of the Russian Army.

PUBLISHING'S NOTE

NOTE ABOUT BOOK PRINTING BEFORE 1925

LICENSES COMMONS

ACKNOWLEDGEMENTS

A Special Thanks to NYPL and other institutions for their kindly permission to use some images of his archives, collections or books used in our book.

Title: **UNIFORMS OF RUSSIAN ARMY DURING THE YEARS 1825-1855. VOL. 1** - **Under the reign of Nicholas I emperor of Russia between 1825-1855**
By A.V.Viskovatov. Serie edit by Luca S. Cristini. First edition by Soldiershop. July 2017
Cover & Art Design: Luca S. Cristini. Plates re-colorations by Anna Cristini. DTP Francesca Mangano
ISBN code: 978-88-93272599
Published by Soldiershop publishing, via Padre Davide, 7 - 24050 Zanica (BG) ITALY. www.soldiershop.com

UNIFORMS
OF THE RUSSIAN ARMY
DURING THE YEARS
1825-1855
VOL. 1

UNDER THE REIGN OF NICHOLAS I EMPEROUR OF
RUSSIA BETWEEN 1825 AND 1855

HISTORICAL DESCRIPTION OF THE CLOTHING AND ARMS
OF THE RUSSIAN ARMY - A.V. VISKOVATOV
(First English translation by Mark Conrad)

Soldiershop is glad to presents the complete collection of the great job made by A.V. Viskovatov dedicated to the uniforms and weapons belonging from the first Zar and Russian emperors to the Russian army during the Napoleonic period, until 1860 about. The time we considered in this volume corresponds to the reigns of Catherine the Great (Catherine II) who reigned since 1762 until his murder on the 6 November 1796.

Our reprint in based on the original 19th century volumes, to be precise the volumes from 4 to 6 are dedicated to the reign of Catherine II; this part is distributed on 3 or 4 volumes.

Our new edition, the first ever published in English, both on paper and digital format, boasts a large number of color plates, many of them unpublished and re-coloured by our team of expert artists and scholars of uniformology. Each volume is based on 100 color plates or more, always accompanied by the original translated text which describes the subjets of the plates.

A unique work in its genre, a must have in any respecting collection!

Aleksandr Vasilevich Viskovatov born 22 April (4 May New Style) 1804, died 27 February (11 March) 1858 in St. Petersburg, Russian military historian. He graduated from the 1st Cadet Corps and served in the artillery, the hydrographic depot of the Naval Ministry, and then in the Department of Military Educational Institutions.

He mainly studied historical artifacts and the histories of military units. Viskovatov's greatest work was the Historical Description of the Clothing and Arms of the Russian Army (Vols. 1-30, St. Petersburg, 1841-62; 2nd ed. Vols. 1-34, St. Petersburg - Novosibirsk - Leningrad, 1899-1948). This work is based on a great quantity of archival documents and contains four thousand colored illustrations.

Viskovatov was the author of Chronicles of the Russian Army (Books 1-20, St. Petersburg, 1834-42) and Chronicles of the Russian Imperial Army (Parts 1-7, St. Petersburg, 1852). He collected valuable material on the history of the Russian navy which went into A Short Overview of Russian Naval Campaigns and General Voyages to the End of the XVII Century (St. Petersburg, 1864; 2nd edition Moscow, 1946). Together with A.I. Mikhailovskii-Danilevskii he helped prepare and create the Military Gallery in the Winter Palace.

He wrote the historical military inscriptions for the walls of the Hall of St. George in the Great Palace of the Kremlin. (From the article in the Soviet Military Encyclopedia.)

CONTENTS

*

Preface pag. 5

*

HISTORICAL DESCRIPTION OF THE CLOTHING AND ARMS OF THE RUSSIAN ARMY
Grenadiers and Infantry 1825-1855

CHANGES IN THE UNIFORM AND ARMS OF THE ARMY FROM 20 NOVEMBER, 1825, TO 18 FEBRUARY, 1855:

1 - GRENADIER REGIMENTS (GRENADERSKIE POLKI).

21 December 1825 - His Royal Highness Prince Eugene of Württemberg's Grenadier Regiment [*Grenaderskii Ego Korolevskago Vysochestva Printsa Yevgeniya Virtembergskago polk*], renamed from the Taurica Grenadier Regiment [*Tavricheskii Grenaderskii polk*], is to replace the letter *T* on epaulettes and shoulder straps [*epolety i plechevye pogony*] with a monogram [*venzel*] made up of the letters *P.*, *E.*, and *W.*, all under a crown (Illus. 1) [813].

11 January 1826 - Prince Paul of Mecklenburg's Grenadier Regiment [*Grenaderskii Printsa Pavla Meklenburgskago polk*], renamed from the Moscow Grenadier Regiment [*Moskovskii Grenaderskii polk*], is to replace the letter *M.* with a monogram of the letters *P.* and *M.* under a crown (Illus. 2) [814].

11 February 1826 - Officers and lower ranks of all Grenadier regiments except those in the Separate Lithuania Corps [*Otdelnyi Litovskii Korpus*], which is to say the Samogitia and Lutsk regiments, are given single-breasted **coats** [*mundiry*] instead of double-breasted, with nine flat [*ploskii*] buttons in front, red cuff flaps [*rukavnye klapany*] instead of dark-green, and red piping down the front, from the center to the tails, and additionally for officers, on the folds of the pockets (Illus. 3, 4, and 5). The former officers' grey riding-trousers [*reituzy*, from Ger. *Reithose*] and white pants [*pantalony*] with high boots [*sapogi*] and the lower ranks' same white pants but with knee gaiters [*kragi*] are replaced with long, dark-green **pants** with red piping on the side seams. Lower ranks at all times, and company-grade officers [*ober-ofitsery*] only in formation and on parade, wear black cloth **half-gaiters** [*polushtiblety*] under these pants and over the boots, fastened with five or six small brass buttons (Illus. 3 and 5). Along with this change, the horizontal **belt for the knapsack** [*poperechnyi rantsevyi remen*] is to be between the two lower buttons on the front of the coat, while the **greatcoat** [*shinel*] is carried on the knapsack [*ranets*] rolled into a tube in its special oilskin case made of raven's-duck [*ravenduchnaya kleenka*] (Illus. 3). Generals, field-grade officers [*shtab-ofitsery*], and adjutants are to have **boots** [*sapogi*] with the **spurs** driven in [*pribivnye spory*]. The **Samogitia and Lutsk regiments** receive the same pants, half-gaiters, and knapsacks as the other Grenadiers, but the first-named item with yellow piping instead of red. In regard to all else they keep the previous uniform (Illus. 6) [815].

10 May 1826 - Generals, field-grade officers, and adjutants, when mounted in formation [*v stroyu*] during the summer, are to wear **white linen pants** [*belyya polotnyanyya pantalony*] without integral spats [*kozyrki*], of the same pattern as previously prescribed for the dark-green ones (Illus. 7). In addition, **suede pants** [*zamshevyya pantalony*] of the same pattern may be worn instead of the linen pants [816].

15 September 1826 - Lower ranks who have completed the regulation number of years of faultless service and have the right to be discharged but who voluntarily remain on active duty are to wear a **gold galloon chevron** [*nashivka iz zolotnago galuna*] on the left sleeve above and in addition to the yellow tape chevron [*nashivka iz zheltago basona*] prescribed on 29 March 1825 [817].

1 January 1827 - Officers' epaulettes are to have little forged or stamped **stars** [*kovannyya zvezdochki*] as rank distinctions, regardless of monograms or letters. These will be silver for gold epaulettes and gold for silver ones [as in the Samogitia and Lutsk Regiments]. Ensigns [*praporshchiki*] will have one (Illus. 8a), sub-lieutenants [*podporuchiki*], majors [*maiory*], and major-generals [*general-maiory*] will have two (Illus. 8b), lieutenants [*poruchiki*], lieutenant-colonels [*podpolkovniki*], and lieutenant-generals [*general-leitenanty*] will have three (Illus. 8c), and staff-captains [*shtabs-kapitany*] (Illus. 8d) will have four, on each epaulette. Captains [*kapitany*], colonels [*polkovniki*], and full generals [*generaly*] are not to have any stars (Illus. 8e) [818].

31 July 1827 - Numbers and letters on the **covers** for shakos and pouches [*kivernye i sumochnye chekhly*] are changed from yellow cloth to yellow oilpaint [*maslyanaya kraska*] [819].

7 March 1828 - Lower ranks who return to their regiments from the Model Infantry Regiment [*Obraztsovyi Pekhotnyi polk*] are to wear a **yellow tape** [*zheltyi bason*] around their shoulder straps (Illus. 9a), while those who have been in Instructional Carabineer Regiments [*Uchebnye Karabinernye polki*] prior to coming from the Model Infantry Regiment are to wear an additional cross strip of yellow tape [*zheltyi basonnyi pogonchik*] with two red stripes (Illus. 9b) [820].

24 March 1828 - The **coats** of lower ranks are not to be tailored with cinches [*peretyazhki*] [821].

24 April 1828 - The following changes were made in articles of uniform and accouterments:

1) A new model **shako** [*kiver*] is introduced, 9 5/8 inches high with a top diameter not less than 9 7/8 inches and not more than 10 1/2 inches. The lower diameter will be the size of the head. The thickness of the upper, lacquered edge is 1/2 inch. (Illus. 10, 11, and 12.)

2) The **shako plate** [*gerb*] will be brass as before, depicting a double-headed eagle with a shield below on which a single-flame grenade is hammered in relief [*vypuklo vybita*], and on this is cut out a number (Illus 12 and 13): in the Emperor of Austria's Regiment — *1*, King of Prussia's — *2*, Graf Arakcheev's — *3*, Hereditary Prince of Prussia's — *4*, Kiev — *5*, Prince Eugene of Württemberg's — *6*, Yekaterinoslav — *7*, Prince Paul of Mecklenburg's — *8*, Siberia — *9*, Graf Rumyantsov's — *10*, Prince Suvorov's — *11*, Astrakhan — *12*, Kherson — *13*, Georgia — *14*, Samogitia — *15*, and Lutsk — *16*. Regiments which possess badges of distinction [*znaki otlichiya*], namely the Emperor of Austria's, King of Prussia's, Hereditary Prince of Prussia's, Graf Arakcheev's, Kiev, Prince Eugene of Württemberg's, Yekaterinoslav, Prince Paul of Mecklenburg's, the Siberia, Graf Rumyantsov of the Trans-Danube's, and Astrakhan, receive new pattern badges in the form of a scroll with the cut-out inscription "*za otlichie*" ["for excellence"] (Illus. 12 and 13) completely covering it, and with its lower edge even with the lower edge of the pompon [*repeika* — literally "little turnip" — M.C.] (Illus. 12).

3) The **shako cords** [*etishket*] are also of a new pattern, consisting of a white cord around the top of the shako and tassels with bows [*banty*] hanging down on the right even with the lower edge of the shako. For privates these last are completely white and for non-commissioned officers white with orange and black (Illus. 12).

4) The **pouch belt** [*perevyaz*] and **sword-belt** [*portupeya*] are prescribed to be 3 1/2 inches wide; the **shoulder belts for the knapsack** [*rantsevye plechevye remni*] — 2 5/8 inches; and the **belt across the chest** [*nagrudnyi remen*] — 2 inches.

5) **Knapsacks** are to be of calfskin [*telyachaya kozha*] as before but with black leather trim (Illus. 10). The knapsack is prescribed to be 15 3/4 inches broad, 14 inches high, and 4 3/8 inches wide. The length of the cover from the upper edge is 10 1/2 inches.

6) In place of their grey coats [*mundiry*], all **non-combatant non-commissioned officers** are issued with dark-green **frock coats** [*syurtuki*] with a single row of buttons and the same collar, cuffs, and shoulder straps as for combatant personnel. **Pants**, however, are grey with red piping on the side seams (Illus. 7) **Non-combatant craftsmen** [*masterovye*] of the lower ranks, as well as medical orderlies [*lazaretnye sluzhiteli*] are to replace their coats with grey cloth **jackets** [*kurtki*] modeled on the coat. Pants are to be as for the non-combatants above (Illus. 14) [822].

27 June 1828 - The Kherson and Georgia [*Gruzinskii*] Grenadier regiments are awarded **badges of distinction** for their shakos [823].

18 May 1829 - Non-commissioned officers who have been recommended by higher command for promotion to officer rank by virtue of years of service are to have **silver sword knots** [*serebryanye temlyaki*] [824].

10 August 1829 - The Grenadier regiments of the Separate Caucasus Corps [*Otdelnyi Kavkazskii Korpus*], the Kherson and the Georgia [*Gruzinskii*], are to replace the shako [*kiver*] with a **headdress** [*shapka*] of black sheepskin [*ovchina*] with a leather peak and accoutered like the Grenadier shakos (Illus. 15 and 16), the only change being a round pompon [*pompon*] in place of the plume [*sultan*]. This pompon is silver for officers and woolen for lower ranks; in the Grenadier platoon [*Grenaderskii vzvod*] of the 1st battalion — red, in the Marksmen [*Strelkovyi vzvod*] platoon — yellow, in the Fusilier companies — white; in the Grenadier platoon of the 2nd battalion — red with light blue below, in the Marksmen platoon — yellow with light blue below, in the Fusilier companies — white with light blue below; and in the Grenadier platoon of the 3rd battalion — red with green below, in the Marksmen platoon — yellow with green below, in the Fusilier companies — white with green below [825].

16 December 1829 - The red **cuffs** of officers' frock coats are changed to dark green with red piping [Illus. 17] [826].

26 December 1829 - All combatant ranks are directed to have the **buttons** on their coats, frock coats, and greatcoats made with the raised image of a grenade with the same number as on the shako plate [827].

20 August 1830 - Officers' rapiers [*shpagi*] are replaced with **half-sabers** [*polusabli*] with black scabbards and brass mountings (Illus. 18 and 19) [828].

9 May 1831 - The **Samogitia** and **Lutsk** Grenadier regiments are directed to have the same uniform as the other Grenadier regiments, which is to say that the plastron is abolished, yellow cloth is changed to red, and white buttons and trim are changed to yellow [829].

1 January 1832 - Generals who have the diamond-studded gold swords [*shpagi*] "*za khrabost*" ["for courage"] are not to use **sword knots** [830].

8 June 1832 - Officers are permitted to wear **moustaches** [831].

3 January 1833 - **Half-gaiters** [*polushtiblety*] are abolished for both company-grade officers and lower ranks (Illus. 20 and 21). Non-commissioned officers and lower ranks are no longer to use **covers** for their shakos or cartridge pouches. Swordknots [*temlyaki*] are abolished for lower ranks except for those non-commissioned officers who have them in silver [832].

20 January 1833 - **Covers for shakos** are restored as before [833].

28 January 1833 - Grenadier regiments (with the exception of the Emperor of Austria's and the King of Prussia's regiments which join the guard infantry) are to have **numbers** on the shako plates and buttons as follows: the Hereditary Prince of Prussia's Regiment — 1, Graf Arakcheev's — 2, Samogitia — 3, Kiev — 4, Prince Eugene of Württemberg's — 5, the Yekaterinoslav — 6, Siberia — 7, Graf Rumyantsov of the Trans-Danube's — 8, and Generalissimus Prince Suvorov's — 9 [834].

20 February 1833 - All combatant ranks are given new pattern **summer pants** [*pantalony*] or **breeches** [*bryuki*], without buttons or integral spats [*kozyrki*] (Illus. 22) [835].

22 February 1833 - Field and company-grade officers are not to use the hat [*shlyapa*], but rather use the **shako** at all times. Regimental and battalion commanders, junior field-grade officers, and adjutants are permitted to have riding horses with **long tails** [836].

14 March 1833 - On the reorganization of Grenadier regiments from three battalions to four, Grenadier and Fusilier privates [*ryadovye*] are assigned **lower pompons** [*repeiki*] in the following colors:

1st battalion: Grenadiers — red, Marksmen — yellow, Fusiliers — white with a green center.

2nd battalion: Grenadiers — black with red below, Marksmen — black with yellow below; Fusiliers — white with a black center.

3rd battalion: Grenadiers — red with light blue below, Marksmen — yellow with light blue below, Fusiliers — light blue with a white center.

4th battalion: Grenadiers — light blue with red below, Marksmen — light blue with yellow below, Fusiliers — white with a light blue center [837].

5 May 1833 - Instead of being cut out, the numbers on the **shako plates** are to be made of tin for lower ranks and silver plated for officers, and are to be fixed on (Illus. 23) [838].

15 July 1833 - Upon the change in the organization of Grenadier regiments, lower ranks are directed to have **forage caps** [*furazhnyya shapki*] with the following colors of piping:

1st battalion: Grenadier platoon — upper and lower (above the band) piping red; Marksmen platoon — upper piping red, lower yellow; 1st, 2nd, and 3rd Fusilier companies — upper piping red.

2nd battalion: Grenadier platoon — upper piping yellow; lower red; Marksmen platoon — upper and lower piping yellow; 4th, 5th, and 6th Fusilier companies — upper piping yellow.

3rd battalion: Grenadier platoon — upper piping light green, lower red; Marksmen platoon — upper piping light green, lower yellow; 7th, 8th, and 9th Fusilier companies — upper piping light green.

4th battalion: Grenadier platoon — upper piping light blue, lower red; Marksmen platoon — upper piping light blue, lower yellow; 10th, 11th, and 12th Fusilier companies — upper piping light blue.

The crown of the forage cap is left dark green as before, with a red band with company numbers cut out of yellow cloth: in the 1st Grenadier company — Cyrillic *1 G.R.* [for "*Grenaderskaya Rota*" — M.C.], in the 1st Fusilier company — Cyrillic *1 R.*, in the 2nd Fusilier company — *2 R.*, and so on. The upper diameter of the cap is to be 10 1/2 inches while the lower is to be according to the size of the head. The height of the band is 1 1/3 inches, and the distance from the band to the top is 2 5/8 inches [839].

29 January 1834 - **His Royal Highness. the Hereditary Prince of Orange's Grenadier Regiment** [*Grenaderskii Ego*

Korolevskago Vysochestva Naslednago Printsa Oranskago polk], renamed from the Kiev Grenadier Regiment, is to have the letters *E.* and *o.* on epaulettes and shoulder straps, with a crown above (Illus. 24) [840].

21 March 1834 - The **Georgia Grenadier Regiment** is to have the number 10 on shako plates and buttons. Upon the reorganization from three battalions to four, the **upper and lower pompons** are to be the following colors:

a) *Lower pompons [repeiki]:*

1st battalion: Grenadiers - red, Marksmen - yellow, Fusiliers - white with a green center.

2nd battalion: Grenadiers - black with red below, Marksmen - black with yellow below, Fusiliers - white with black below.

3rd battalion: Grenadiers - red with light blue below, Marksmen - yellow with light blue below, Fusiliers - light blue with a white center.

4th battalion: Grenadiers - light blue with red below, Marksmen - light blue with yellow below, Fusiliers - white with a light blue center.

b) *Upper pompons [pompony]:*

1st battalion: Grenadiers - red, Marksmen - yellow, Fusiliers - white.

2nd battalion: Grenadiers - black with red below, Marksmen - black with yellow below, Fusiliers - black with white below.

3rd battalion: Grenadiers - red with light blue below, Marksmen - yellow with light blue below, Fusiliers - white with light blue below.

4th battalion: Grenadiers - light blue with red below, Marksmen - light blue with yellow below, Fusiliers - light blue with white below [841].

2 May 1834 - The **Rostov Grenadier Regiment**, renamed from the Graf Arakcheev's Grenadier Regiment, is to have the Cyrillic letter *R.* on epaulettes and shoulder straps [842].

26 September 1834 - Lower ranks are directed to wear the **knapsack** on two belts lying crosswise over the chest (Illus. 25) [843].

14 June 1835 - **Prince Frederick of the Netherlands' Grenadier Regiment** [*Grenaderskii Printsa Fridrikha Niderlandskago polk*], renamed from the Rostov Grenadier Regiment, is to replace the letter *P.* on epaulettes and shoulder straps with a monogram of the letters *P. F.* and *N.* under a crown (Illus. 26) [844].

15 July 1833 - In the **Siberia Grenadier Regiment** shoulder straps are to have the two Cyrillic letters *S.* and *G.* instead of the single letter *S* [845].

20 August 1835 - It is ordered that:

1) Officers wear the **knapsack** using only two shoulder belts without any horizontal strap over the chest. These belts are to be lacquered (Illus. 27).

2) For lower ranks a **linen case** [*kholshchevyi chekhol*] or pocket [*karman*] for the forage cap is to be put on the outside of the knapsack on the side that lies on the soldier's back. These cases are to be made from the linings of wornout coats.

3) For drummers the **knapsack** is to have one belt as before, worn over the left shoulder [846].

31 January 1836 - The lower ranks' **greatcoat** [*shinel*] is to have nine buttons instead of ten, namely: six along the front opening, two on the shoulder straps, and one on the flap behind [847].

4 April 1836 - In the fifth battalions of the Grenadier Corps **lower pompons** are to be: Grenadier platoon — red with green, Marksmen platoon — yellow with green, Fusilier companies — green with a white center. In the Georgia Grenadier Regiment the lower pompons in the fifth battalion are to be the same as prescribed for the foregoing regiments, while the upper pompons are: Grenadier platoon — red with green, Marksmen platoon — yellow with green, Fusilier companies white with green below. Piping on the forage caps in the fifth battalions of all Grenadier regiments is to be: Grenadier platoon — white above, red below; Marksmen platoon — white above, yellow below; Fusilier companies — white above [848].

27 April 1836 - **Pompons** are to be lined with black leather [849].

13 May 1836 - Girths [*podprugi*] for officers' saddles are to be dark green with red stripes [850].

21 October 1836 - Shako plumes [*kivernye sultany*] are to be 19 1/4 inches high from the triangular socket to the top, with an upper circumference of 10 inches and a lower one of 7. Its weight is to be not more than 8 1/10 ounces [851].

14 January 1837 - Handles of **entrenching tools** [*shantsovyi instrument*] are no longer to be painted with oil-based paint, but rather the wood is to be varnished [*pokryvat lakom*]. Directives for carrying these tools are as follows:

"For fitting the ax, spade, pick, and mattock to the strap on which the sword-belt clasp is sewn, a sheath is formed through which the strap on which the said articles are to be held is passed. These are fitted as follows:

1) "Ax [*topor*] — attach with the blade below the pouch; on the side of the ax cover that is turned toward the body, 1 1/4 inches from the sharp edge, sew a black strap 1 1/8 inches wide and pass it through the sheath formed by the strap on which is sewn the sword-belt clasp. Fasten it with an iron buckle of the same size as used for the knapsack. The buckle is sewn slightly slanted onto the outside of the axhead cover, so that the corner of this buckle is not higher than the axhead cover'" (Illus. 28).

2) "Spade [*lopatka*] — Sew a black leather strap, 1 1/8 inches wide, to the right side of the back of the spade cover ; on the same side of the cover, but on the left, sew an iron buckle of the same size as used for the knapsack . This strap is attached with two stitchings; one even with the top of the cover and the other at the end of the strap, 1 3/4 inches from the top of the cover and 14/3 inches [sic, "8/3 *vershka*" — M.C.] from the side. The strap is passed through the sheath formed by the strap on which the sword-belt clasp is sewn, and is fastened to a buckle sewn onto the left of the cover and placed appropriately for the strap" (Illus. 28).

3) "Mattock [*motyga*] — On the face of the mattock cover, 2 5/8 inches from its pointed end and using one stitching, sew a black, 1 1/8-inch wide strap, leaving 1 3/4 inches of its end free. Cut a slit across the width of this free end through which the strap, after being wrapped around the mattock, is then pulled and passed through the sheath formed by the strap on which the sword-belt clasp is sewn, fastening to an iron buckle of the same size as used for the knapsack. This buckle is sewn to the cover of the blunt end of the mattock, next to the handle, and is not to be any higher than the cover of the blunt end of the mattock" (Illus. 29).

4) "The pick [*kirka*] is to be carried in exactly the same way as the mattock"(Illus. 29).

"In addition to these fittings, there is an ear-like tab [*ushko*], made from a 1 1/8-inch wide strap, on the pouch-belt halfway between the shoulder strap and the pouch [but 4 3/8 inches above the pouch for the ax). This tab is for attaching the handles of the spade, ax, mattock, and pick, and is finished in white for those troops who have white equipment and in black for those who have black equipment. An entrenching tool with such a fitting is carried in the following manner: the handle is inserted through the tab that is fixed to the crossbelt, and the tool is laid with the back of the cover toward the frog of the sword-belt; the strap that is sewn to the cover is passed through the sheath between the frog and the clasp, fastened to the buckle on the cover, pushed through the little loop, and bent under so that the bend is at the 5/8-inch point. The tool is fitted so that its cover does not touch the body of the pouch [852]".

15 July 1837 - Officers are given a new pattern of **sash** [*sharf*] that instead of the previous wide lace has narrow, silver lace with three stripes of light-orange and black silk, and is with its entire width between the two lower buttons of the coat (Illus. 30) [853].

17 December 1837 - In order to introduce uniformity to officers' **epaulettes**, a new pattern is confirmed with the addition of a fourth, narrow braid [*uzkii vitok*] (Illus. 31) [854].

17 January 1838 - In summer, regimental **staff-hornists** [*shtab-gornisty*], when mounted in formation, are to wear winter trousers [*bryuki*]. Instead of knapsacks they are to have valises [*chemodany*] of the cavalry pattern. Their horses are to be with bridles [*uzdechki*] and have a saddle patterned after the one for mounted artillerymen, without a shabraque or saddlecloth [*cheprak ili val'trap*] [855].

16 August 1838 - **Archduke Francis-Charles' Grenadier Regiment** [*Grenaderskii Erts-Gertsoga Frantsa-Karla polk*], renamed from the Samogitia Grenadier Regiment, is to have a monogram on epaulettes and shoulder straps made of the letters *F.* and *K.* under a crown (Illus. 32) [856].

4 January 1839 - Generals and field and company-grade officers are not to have any bows or bands [*banty*] on the front of their **pants** or **trousers**. These are to be worn completely smooth in the manner prescribed for lower ranks [857].

16 March 1839 - Lower ranks' **pouch-belts** [*perevyazi*] and **sword-belts** [*portupei*], which were at first 3 7/8 inches wide and then, since 1828, 3 inches wide, are to be 2 3/5 inches wide with strips 1/5 inch from the edge. **Drummers' crossbelts** [*barabannyya perevyazi*] are as before, 4 2/5 inches wide [858].

15 September 1839 - As His Imperial Highness Grand Duke CONSTANTINE NIKOLAEVICH [*Ego Imperatorskoe Vysochestvo Velikii Knyaz KONSTANTIN NIKOLAEVICH*] is the Honorary Colonel [*Shef*] of the **Georgia Grenadier Regiment** [*Gruzinskii Grenaderskii polk*], the collars and cuff flaps of officers' coats in this regiment are directed to have gold lace bars [*petlitsy*] [859].

26 May 1840 - Epaulettes and shoulder straps in **His Majesty the King of Prussia's Grenadier Regiment** [*Grenaderskii Ego Velichestva Korolya Prusskago polk*] are to have a new monogram made of the letters F., W., and R. (Illus. 33), and officers are to have gold lace bars on their coats [860].

9 September 1840 - His Imperial Highness the Hereditary Tsesarevich's Yekaterinoslav Grenadier Regiment [*Yekaterinoslavskii Grenaderskii Ego Imperatorskago Vysochestva Naslednika Tsesarevicha polk*] is to have the monogram of His Highness under a crown on epaulettes and shoulder straps (Illus. 34) and gold lace bars on the collars and cuff flaps of officers' coats [861].

16 October 1840 - Lower ranks who have earned the right to discharge on indefinite leave [*bezrochnyi otpusk*] but who voluntarily remain on active service are to wear **gold galloon chevrons** [*shevrony ili nashivki, iz zolotago galuna*]on the left sleeve, one for every five years of extra service. On this same basis these same chevrons are given to non-commissioned officers who have declined promotion to officer rank and are receiving two-thirds of an ensign's pay for serving five or more years after declining such promotion [862].

23 January 1841 - The capes [*bolshie vorotniki*] of officers' **greatcoats** are to be 28 inches long as measured from the lower edge of the collar [*malyi vorotnik*] [863].

26 November 1842 - Until a new uniform is approved, officers and lower ranks of the Georgia Grenadier Regiment and the Erivan Carabinier Regiment are to wear **forage caps** in place of the sheepskin headdress [864].

["The Circassians deserve the character of excellent marksmen, and the **Russian officers** are the first victims of their skill. These perish in very considerable number, a number, indeed, quite disproportionate to that of the soldiers. It has frequently been found necessary to make them wear the great coat of the latter to save them from the enemy's balls; but this precaution is repugnant to their valour; and, while it is but optional, they not only disdain it, but even make a ostentatious display in their dress. The **white cap** is the one which they prefer, and a **close coat of damask** of the country in their habitual costume. Discipline allows them full latitude on this point." *Russia Under the Autocrat Nicholas the First.* Ivan Golovine, 1846. Vol. 2, page 325.]

["'Kill the blacks,' said the Turks, meaning the Russian Officers, 'and it will be all up with the grays (the soldiers.)'" *Russia Under the Autocrat Nicholas the First.* Ivan Golovine, 1846. Vol. 2, page 310.]

8 April 1843 - Officers and combatant lower ranks are given a new model **shako** [*kiver*], 8 1/3 inches high and curving slightly inward toward the bottom. New dimensions are prescribed for the shako **plumes**: 17 inches high from the socket to the top, an upper circumference of 9 1/4 inches, and a lower circumference of 6 1/8 inches (Illus. 35 and 36) [865].

Together with this, **rank distinctions** for lower ranks in the form of trim sewn onto shoulder straps [*nashivki na plechevykh pogonakh*] are established as follows:

1) For sergeants [*feldfebeli*] — wide gold galloon, sewn in one row across the shoulder strap, close to the button hole (Illus. 37a).

2) For distinguished officer candidates [*portupei-praporshchiki*] and officer candidates [*podpraporshchiki*] — narrow gold galloon around the edge of the shoulder straps (Illus. 37b).

3) For section non-commissioned officers [*otdelennye unter-ofitsery*] —narrow wool tape [*bason*], white with a red stripe down the center, in three rows across the shoulder strap (Illus. 37c).

4) For other non-commissioned officers [*prochie unter-ofitsery*] — the same tape, sewn on the same but in two rows (Illus. 38a).

5) For lance-corporals [*yefreitory*] — the same tape, sewn on the same but in one row (Illus. 38b) [866].

8 April 1843 - In order to more easily be distinguished from field-grade officers' epaulettes, it is directed that **drum-majors' epaulettes** [*tambur-mazhorskie epolety*] have red silk mixed in the gold braided threads and in the hanging fringe (Illus. 39) [867].

10 May 1843 - The covers of the **cartridge-pouches** [*patronnyya sumki*] are not to have any break on top [*bez pereloma vverkhu*], and are to measure [with the cover sewn onto the body of the pouch]: length — 8 3/4 inches, width at the top edge — 9 5/8 inches, width at the bottom edge — 10 1/2 inches [868].

2 June 1843 - The method of fitting the **shako plate and badge** for distinction to the shako is confirmed, according to which the lower edge of the shako plate, with or without the badge of distinction, is to lie at the point halfway across the width of the lacquered shako strap, with the cross on the crown in the plate lying on the lower edge of the badge for distinction. The badge for distinction itself is to be even with the top of the shako (Illus. 36) [869].

2 January 1844 - Officers are to have an oblong, metal **cockade** [*kokarda*] on the band of their forage caps, in the same colors as the cockade on officers' hats (Illus. 40) [870].

8 January 1844 - Staff-hornists [*shtab-gornisty*], when mounted in formation, are permitted to have spurs [871].

8 May 1844 - It is directed that shakos [*kivera*] be replaced by **helmets** [*kaski*] of black lacquered leather, with two visors (front and back), brass (gilt for officers) mountings on top of and behind the crown, and, on top of the upper mountings, a tube with two round openings in the sides, which, when desired, can be opened or closed by turning the tube. To the top of the tube, closing it, is soldered an ornamentation in the form of a single-flamed grenade, into which a black, horsehair plume [*sultan*] is placed, held to the tube by means of a screw passing into the interior of the tube. The screw's upper, outer part ends in a small, round part in the form of a convex button. These helmets are to have the same plate, chin-scales, and badge for distinction as were on the shakos (Illus. 41 and 42). Generals and field and company-grade officers are to wear the chin-scales of the helmet fastened over the front visor, and are to use the helmet in place of the hat when wearing the coat (with plume) (Illus. 43) or the frock coat (Illus. 44). In campaign dress the helmet is likewise to be worn without the plume, as is also the case for training, guard mounts, and parades that take place within the unit [872].

20 May 1844 - A new scheme for lower ranks' **forage caps** is approved, on the basis of which the piping on the upper edge is to be: in the 1st battalion — red, in the 2nd — white, in the 3rd — light blue, in the 4th — yellow, and in the 5th — dark green. The cap band remains as before, red with numbers and Cyrillic letters cut out of yellow cloth: in the 1st Grenadier company - 1.G.R., in the 1st Fusilier company - 1.R., and so on, as previously. For officers of all battalions the cap band and piping on the top edge are red [873].

30 June 1844 - **His Imperial Highness MICHAEL PAVLOVICH'S Grenadier Regiment** [*Grenaderskii Ego Imperatorskago Vysochestva MIKHAILA PAVLOVICHA polk*], renamed from the Siberia Grenadier Regiment, is to have the monogram of His Highness under a crown on epaulettes and shoulder straps (Illus. 45), and the collars and cuff flaps of officers' coats are to have gold lace bars [874].

17 November 1844 - Instructions for storing and protecting the **helmet plume** [*kasochnyi sultan*] are approved: "When lower ranks are on campaign and must wear helmets without plumes, the plumes are to be kept in the greatcoat cases. If personnel are wearing their coats [*mundiry*], then the plume is to be laid in the middle of the greatcoat before it is rolled up so that the small, round fitting is on one side even with the edge of the greatcoat while the strands lie smoothly stretched out to the other side across the width of the roll. If personnel are wearing their greatcoats, then the plume is rolled up in the coat [*mundir*] in the same manner. When wearing both the greatcoat and the coat, then the plume is to be simply laid in the greatcoat case which always remains on top of the knapsack. So that the plume keeps a good appearance in any case, however, it is necessary that upon removing it from the helmet, its strands be gathered so that the round fitting is on the outside and that they be tied with a thread about 5 inches below the round fitting [875]."

7 December 1844 - Generals who are wearing a regimental coat [*polkovoi mundir*] when not on duty are to have a **white plume** [*sultan*] on the hat [*shlyapa*] instead of a black one [876].

4 January 1845 - Officers' helmets are to have, on the right side under the chin-scales, a metal **cockade** patterned after the one worn on the hat [Illus. 46] [877].

9 August 1845 - The **plume** is not to be worn with camp dress [*pre lagernoi forme*], even if those personnel entitled to plumes are wearing coats [*mundiry*] [878].

26 April 1846 - Instead of a brass spear point, **unit guidons** [*zhalonerskie znaki*, from Fr. *jalonner* — M.C.] are to have a brass ball [879].

23 June 1846 - Upon the introduction of percussion-lock weapons in the infantry (Illus. 47), the following description for fitting the **firing-cap pouch** [*kapsyulnaya sumka*] is approved for all troops:
In the infantry the cap pouch is fastened to the cartridge-pouch crossbelt. For this a small, black, rectangular strap is sewn obliquely to the back of the pouch, 3 1/4 inches wide and 2 5/8 inches high, with two buttonholes in the top corners, cut 1/2 inch from the edges. The left end of this stitching must be at least 1/4 inch below the top edge of the pouch, and its middle at least 7/8 inch from the bottom of the pouch. Two leather buttons are sewn below on the crossbelt, placed appropriately for the buttonholes of the pouch strap. When the pouch strap is fastened to the crossbelt, the lower edge of the belt must be directly against the stitching of the pouch strap. The pouch must be on the right side of the soldier's chest, 1 3/4 inches from a line passing from the collar opening through the center of the chest, and the top straight edge of the attached pouch must be horizontal and opposite the third button from the top of the coat (Illus. 48 and 49) [880].

9 January 1848 - On those days when they are obliged to remain in ceremonial dress [*prazdnichnaya forma*] after the mounting of the guard [*posle razvoda*], generals and field and company-grade officers are permitted to wear the **frock coat** with helmet and plume for walking-out (Illus. 50) [881].

28 March 1848 - On the occasion of the Georgia Grenadier Regiment being retitled **His Imperial Highness the Grand Duke CONSTANTINE NIKOLAEVICH'S Grenadier Regiment** [*Grenaderskii Ego Imperatorskago Vysochestva Velikago Knyazya KONSTANTINA NIKOLAEVICHA polk*], field and company-grade officers and lower ranks of this Regiment are directed to have the cipher of His Highness on epaulettes and shoulder straps, according to the pattern specially approved by HIGHEST authority, in gold for field and company-grade officers and in red cloth for lower ranks (Illus. 51) [(882)].

8 August 1848 - This regiment, concurrently with other infantry troops of the **Separate Caucasus Corps**, is given new uniform and equipment, according to the following description, applicable to all troops:

1.) Instead of the sheepskin hat, a **hat** [*shapka*] in the pattern of the Line cossacks, with a top of dark-green army cloth, and with piping on top in cloth of the same color as the shoulder straps. Officers' shapkas are to be trimmed with lace. These shapkas are not to have plates, grenades, or chin-scales, but badges of distinction are to be fixed to the front (for those troops who are so entitled).

2.) Instead of the coat [*mundir*], a **half-caftan** [*polukaftan*], with collar, shoulder straps, and piping like that now used on the coat. In regiments in which officers have lace bars, they are to have yet another half-caftan without lace bars, and are to wear the one with lace bars only on those occasions on which the coat [*mundir*] is now worn. The half-caftan with lace bars is also to have two bars on the cuffs, as for cossacks. Non-combatants and troops in the train [*furshtat*] are to have half-caftans, *sharavary* [Caucasian trousers — M.C.], and shapkas like combatants', but in grey cloth for those whose uniform is prescribed to be grey.

3.) Instead of winter and summer pants, winter and summer **sharavary pants**.

4.) **Boots** with long shafts, of black Russian leather [*yuft*], for troops on active service in place of the normal third pair.

5.) Instead of the cartridge-pouch and crossbelt, an **ammunition pouch** [*patrontash*] of black Russian leather, with places for 60 rounds, and with a belt of white Russian leather blackened as for jägers.

6.) Instead of the sword-belt, a **waist-belt with frog** [*poyasnoi remen s lopastyu*], according to special pattern, of white Russian leather blackened as for jägers, fastened with a blackened iron belt-plate.

7.) Instead of the calfskin knapsack, a **knapsack** of black Russian leather, meant to last for eight years.

8.) The **straps** for the knapsack are to be white Russian leather in the pattern now used by all troops, but blackened as for jägers.

9.) An iron **cooking pot** [*kotelok*] with lid, to be issued to every third man, to be carried by personnel in the second rank. The other personnel keep the mess tin now in use.

10.) Instead of the short sword [*tesak*] a **sapper's sword** [*sapernyi nozh*] is to be issued to all combatant lower ranks without exception. A sheath for the bayonet is to be made part of the scabbard, according to the dragoon model. The same sapper's sword is to be issued to troops in the Train and to those non-combatant lower ranks who have any kind of weapon, but without the scabbard for the bayonet if the weapon is not a musket.

11.) Officers are to have **half-sabers** with Caucasian shashka blades, but with dragoon hilts, with an exposed sword-belt over the shoulder like that used by His Royal Highness the Hereditary Prince of Württemberg's Dragoon Regiment (ex-Nizhnii Novgorod Dragoons) [*Dragunskii Ego Korolevskago Vysochestva Naslednika Printsa Virtembergskago (byvshii Nizhegorodskii) polk*], trimmed in lace the same color as the buttons. (Illus. 52, 53, 54, 55, 56, 57, 58, and 59.)

Together with this it is directed by HIGHEST AUTHORITY:

1.) In warm weather troops of the Separate Caucasus Corps are allowed to wear **forage caps** with long visors, made from worn-out coats [*mundiry*].

2.) Instead of deerskin [*losinnaya kozha*], **equipment** is to be Russian leather [*yuftovaya kozha*], blackened and waxed [*vychernennaya voskom*], for all troops in the Caucasus Corps. White deerskin equipment now in use is to be blackened for the rest of its service life.

3.) Generals, adjutants, and in general all officers who are in the Caucasus but not on assigned duty [*nesostoyashchie v stroyu*], are to keep the present uniform and headdress.

4.) The **Reserve Division** [*Rezervnaya diviziya*] of the Separate Caucasus Corps is to keep the present normal Army uniform, with the new one to be issued only to those who are permanently sent to the Caucasus.

5.) Troop detachments of the Separate Caucasus Corps are to wear Caucasian uniform when with the Model Infantry Regiment and Model Foot Battery [*Obraztsovyi Pekhotnyi polk i Obraztsovaya Peshaya Batareya*].

The pieces of uniform and other items mentioned here are to be made according to the following descriptions:

Shapka headdress — like that of the Line cossacks, of dark-green army cloth, with cloth piping in the color of the shoulder straps. The body of black sheepskin, with straps tied to it instead of chin-scales. Troops with badges of distinction are to fasten them on the front of the shapka on the wool body.

Half-caftan — dark-green army cloth; collar, shoulder straps, and piping in regimental colors, like those presently on the coat. Cuffs on the sleeves according to pattern, slit, of dark-green cloth with red piping, but without flaps or buttons. The skirts of the half-caftan are slit behind and have flaps on the pockets, without piping. The skirts are sewn to the waist with some small pleating, for fullness below. The half-caftan must be 8 3/4 inches above the knees when worn by a kneeling man. Half-caftans for non-commissioned officers have the present pattern of lace sewn on the collar and cuffs. Buttons: 9 down the front, 2 on the shoulder straps, and 2 at the waist, for a total of 13.

Winter *sharavary* — dark-green army cloth, with pleats in front, three on each side, lined in linen, with a waistband 3 1/2 inches wide in front and 2 5/8 inches wide in back. Length of the sharavary: the back half must be even with the top of the heel of the boot, while the front half is 7/8 inch shorter than the back. The width of the lower part of the sharavary and the side seams are like those of the pants presently being used. Soldiers in the Train and non-combatants who are to have shapkas, half-caftans, and sharavary of grey factory cloth, are to be issued this material, along with the necessary trim, on the same basis of allocation as for combatant lower ranks.

Summer *sharavary* — of army-issue Flemish linen [*flamskoe armeiskoe polotno*], with the same waistband, but 3 inches wide in the front and 1 3/4 inches wide in the back. The length of the sharavary and the width of the lower part are to be the same as for the pants presently in use by the infantry.

High boots [*Sapogi dlinnye*] — of black Russian leather, welted [*rantovye*], with stitched uppers [*prishivnyya golovki*]. When necessary, the boots may be worn over the cloth sharavary, being fastened above the knee by means of a strap and iron buckle.

Knapsack — according to pattern, of black Russian leather, lined in linen, with a raw leather thong for tying the top of the knapsack. The finished knapsack is 19 inches high and 18 3/8 inches wide. The raw thong is 1/4 inch wide and 44 inches long. Straps for the knapsack are white Russian leather, blackened with wax as for jägers. The knapsack has one iron buckle and two iron hooks, and the knapsack straps have two iron rings and two iron buckles.

Greatcoat case — as previously.

Cooking pot — of sheet iron, with cover, tinned on the inside, and with an iron handle. The pot is to be 8 1/8 inches high with lid, 3 3/4 inches wide, and 21 1/4 inches around. The lid is 1 3/4 inches high. The pot with lid weighs 3 pounds while the handle is 2 1/2 ounces. This pot is issued to one out of three men and is to be carried by personnel in the second rank. The other men are to have the steel mess tin presently in use.

Ammunition pouch — according to pattern, of black Russian leather, as is the cover which has a linen lining, with a leather interior lining, places for 60 rounds, and two iron buckles.

Crossbelt for the ammunition pouch — of white Russian leather, 56 inches long, 1 1/3 inches wide, blackened as for jägers.

Waist-belt — with frog and sheath for the sapper sword, of white Russian leather, blackened as for jägers. A blackened iron belt plate with hasp is to be used to fasten this belt in front [883].

23 September 1848 - As a supplement to the changes of 8 August of this year, the following description of the fitting of the **ammunition pouch** and **firing-cap pouch** for the troops of the Separate Caucasus Corps is confirmed: The ammunition pouch is worn on a belt across the left shoulder and on top of the knapsack belts, of a length such that when the soldier is wearing the knapsack, the ammunition pouch in back is 7/8 inch below it and can be freely moved forward from under the right arm. The ends of the belt are passed through loops, one of which is sewn along the left corner of the pouch with its top edge even with the bend of the cover. The other loop is sewn lengthways on the right corner, but slightly slanted. The belt ends are fastened with buckles at the corners of the pouch, on its lower side. The firing-cap pouch, of the same design as that approved for other troops, is tightly fastened to the front side of the ammunition pouch at the far right corner so that its upper edge is even with the upper edge of the ammunition pouch itself, and is located so that it is hidden under the pouch cover [884].

31 October 1848 - As a supplement to these same changes, the following description of the **officers' sword-belt** [*ofitserskaya portupeya*] in the Separate Caucasus Corps is approved, along with the manner of wearing it and the half-saber: "The officers' sword-belt, of black morocco [*safyan*], trimmed with galoon, 7/8 inch wide, and gold or silver according to the color of the buttons, is to be of such a length that the rings to which the slings are attached reach the officer's waist. The front sling [*perednii pasovyi remen*] is 3 1/2 inches long and the back one is 13 1/8 inches. The length of the small strap connecting them depends on the size of the waist and can be 4 inches or longer. On the half-saber's scabbard the mounts and rings through which the slings pass are fitted thus: upper mount — at the very top of the endpiece, which itself is 1 3/4 inches long, lower mount — 8 3/4 inches beneath the upper. The rings themselves are soldered to the ring-mounts not on the curve that follows the edge of the blade, but a third of the way around, on the side of the half-saber that faces the body. The sword-belt is worn over the caftan and under the right epaulette, between the button and small epaulette strap. The front buckle is to be even with the third button from the top. The connecting strap on the left side goes along the waist seam. The rear sling lies on the thigh, while the half-saber, turned blade up, is somewhat in front of the left side of the body, so that the top of the hilt is at the same height as the third coat button from the bottom, and so that its weight is equally supported by both slings. The ends of the sword-belt and slings are passed through the small, adjustable loops provided so that they do not hang loosely." [885].

24 November 1848 - The uniform changes of 8 August of this year are extended to apply to **non-combatants** [*nestroevye*] [886].

14 March 1849 - Officers of the **King of the Netherlands' Grenadier Regiment** [*Grenaderskii Korolya Niderlandskago polk*], (formerly the Kiev then the Prince of Orange's), are to have gold lace bars on the collar and cuffs of the coat and a cipher under a crown on the epaulettes, according to the design approved by HIGHEST authority (Illus. 60) [887].

19 April 1849 - With the introduction of new **English signal bugles** [*Angliiskie signalnye rozhki*] (Illus. 61) in Grenadier regiments and the other infantry, the following directive is to be used when fitting them to their belts, and is applicable to all infantry troops.

1.) The belt for carrying the bugle is cut from old leather equipment, 1 1/4 inches wide, just so long that a bugle hanging from it is even with the wrist of the left hand.

2.) Sew a brass buckle to the lower end of the belt , of the same width as the belt. Fasten the upper end of the belt, passed through the bend of the bugle, to the buckle and pass it under the loop sewn below the buckle, so that it can be seen for 1 1/4 inches.

3.) The small loop, of the same width as the belt, is to be made of the same leather, but the buckle is to be that used by the troops on the current pattern belts since these belts are the same width as the belts prescribed for the English bugles.

4.) Buglers are to wear the belt and bugle over the left shoulder, under the shoulder belt, so that the buckle is on the chest next to the second button of the coat while the bugle is along the right thigh with the mouthpiece up and the bell down (Illus. 62) [888].

14 September 1849- Approval is given as to the type of **percussion pistol** [*udarnyi pistolet*] for generals and field and company-grade officers of Grenadier regiments and other infantry (Illus. 63) [889].

9 November 1849 - The **helmet** is to be wider than previously so that when worn it comes over the upper part of the ears. This applies to all troops with helmets (Illus. 64) [890].

25 November 1849 - HIGHEST Approval is given to the following directive concerning the fitting of the **helmet**:
The helmet is large enough so that the head never suffers discomfort under any circumstances and the lower edges reach the top part of the ear even when large winter earmuffs [*zimnie naushniki*] are worn. The helmet is always worn, though, so that the upper part of the ear is concealed underneath. At the same time, so that the screws holding the chin-scales do not press on the head, the chin-scales are fixed 1/2 inch higher than previously; that is, so that it is 3 inches from the lower edge of the helmet to the top point of the chin-scales (Illus. 64) [891].

25 November 1849 - The sheepskin **shapka** approved on 8 August 1848 for infantry troops of the Separate Caucasus Corps is to be worn a little behind the head and tilted over the right brow, so that the left side of the forehead is obliquely exposed [892].

24 December 1849 - The grip on the hilt of the **gold half-saber** awarded for bravery is to be gold instead of wrapped with black, lacquered leather (Illus. 65) [893].

17 January 1851 - Approval is given to the following description, applicable to all infantry troops, of the manner of gathering up and folding back the skirts [*poly*] of the **greatcoat** when on the march.

a.) The skirts of the greatcoat are gathered up inside and fastened using seven leather buttons or toggles, sewn inside on the lower edge of the skirts, and an equal number of loops sewn on the skirts at the right height so that when buttoned up, the skirts are no lower than the knee. For a better hold, wire hooks instead of toggles may be sewn on the edge of the skirts (Illus. 66).

b.) In hot weather the gathered-up skirts of the greatcoat may also be folded back. For this a leather toggle is sewn inside on one side right at the upwards fold, and another loop is sewn on the other side, long enough so that the skirts can be fastened together when it is folded back (Illus. 67) [894].

8 July 1851 — With the issue to the forces of **percussion weapons** with cases or covers for firing nipples [*sterzhni*], the cover [*polunagalishche*] used up to now is withdrawn. Additionally, approval is given to the patterns and descriptions of the following articles:

a.) **Infantry drum** [*Pekhotnyi baraban*] — the shell [*kadlo*] of the drum is brass (in the same color as the helmet mountings, as previously), cylindrical, 14 inches in diameter but only 9 7/8 inches high. Both of its edges are bent bluntly inward to form a tubing, and when bent are 1/2 inch thick. On the seam of the shell, 5 1/4 inches from the lower edge, there is a small round hole 1/2 inch in diameter.

Drum bracket [*Barabannaya skoba*] — a piece in the same style of brass, 1 1/8 inches wide by 7 inches long , bent so that it is 1 1/4 inches high and 2 1/4 inches long . Its feet, by which it is soldered to the shell, are 1 1/8 inches long and semicircular. This bracket is soldered to the shell below the hole, a little more than 1 3/4 inches from the lower edge. A small circular hole is on the top side of the bracket, and a small rectangular hole is on the bottom side, the same size as the iron screw of which more is said below.

Drum hook [*Barabannyi kryuchek*]— brass, the same color as the shell, with a round, 7/8-inch base, soldered to the shell on the side opposite the bracket, 1 3/4 inches from the lower edge, with the base up.

Drum device [*Barabannyi gerb*] — this is a two-headed eagle of the same size and appearance as on the helmet, pressed into an oval, brass plate (the same color as the shell) with a raised and rounded edge. It is soldered to the center of the shell between the hook and the bracket and is equidistant from both edges of the shell, so that the foot holding the laurel wreath is toward the bracket and the other foot toward the hook. The oval device has a long axis of 7 1/2 inches and a short one of 5 3/4 inches.

Drum screw [*Barabannyi vint*] — iron, 4 1/2 inches long and 1/3 inch across. The end on which the thread is cut is round and 2 inches long. The other end is also round and is bend back into a hook. The nut for this screw is likewise iron and round, two-winged, 1 7/8 inches across and 7/8 inch high.

Drum snares [*Barabannyya struny*] — two, of sheep gut, about 1/8 inch thick and about 19 inches long, with the ends worked into small straps; one end is put through the brass drum hook and the other through the hook of the drum screw, which is inserted through the holes of the drum bracket and there serves to tighten these snares.

Drumheads [*Barabannyya shkury*] — two, unfinished, specially made, trimmed around to a diameter about 5 1/4 inches larger than the shell. The edges of the heads are turned over the hoop stays [*podobruchiki*] — two, semicircular, 1/2-inch thick, wooden, bent to such a diameter that with the heads fitted over them they fit on the shell. The edges of the heads fitted over the hoop stays are painted white or black, according to the color of the leather equipment.

Drum hoops [*Barabannye obruchi*] — of hard, smooth wood, bent round, 1/3 inch thick, 2 inches wide with slightly rounded edges, of a diameter to fit closely onto the shell when fitted with the drumhead. A quarter-inch from the upper edge of the bottom hoop, two elongated rectangular cutouts are made, one across from the other, through which the snares are passed. Above these are ten small, round, equidistant holes, each a little over 7/8 inch in diameter. These holes are made at an angle so that, from the inside, they lead from up to down in the top hoop and from down to up in the bottom one. In both cases the distance from the edges on the side turned toward the shell is no closer than 7/8 inch. These hoops are painted: when black leather equipment is used — all black, and when white equipment is used — white on the inside and in alternating white and black triangles on the outside. The hoops are fitted to the shell so that the holes are not placed directly opposite each other, but alternate.

Drum cord [*Barabanaya verevka*] — plain, pipe-clayed [*peikovaya*], about 1/3 inch thick and 7 feet long. At one end it is fastened to a hole in the bottom hoop right next to the bracket. Then, passing through all the holes by alternating the top and bottom hoops, it goes around the edge of the bottom hoop, where the other end is fixed.

Drum tensioners [*Barabannye bunty*], or loops [*gaiki*], nine in all — of the same leather and color as the rest of the accouterments, 1 3/4 inches high, 1 1/2 inches wide at the top, and 2 inches wide at the bottom. These loops are evenly sewn together, without the small wings that existed previously, and are put on each of the upper turns of the cord with the seams facing the shell, where they can tighten the drumheads as much as necessary. No loop is attached on the turn at the hole in the shell so this hole remains unobstructed.

Drum sling [*Barabannyi pogon*] — leather, of the same appearance as the rest of the equipment, 2 inches wide and about 49 inches long. One end is attached to the top hoop with a small, unfinished strap that by means of two small holes goes through the hoop, about 7/8 inch from the upper edge and to the right of the hole that is located above the bracket. The other end of the sling, turned back under itself and fastened with the same kind of small strap, forms a loop through which is passed the end of the cord that goes around the drum, so that here too the sling stays to the right of the bracket. This sling is fitted so that when the drummer carries the drum slung over his shoulder, his elbow touches the edge of the top hoop. When the drum must be carried on the hook of the sword-belt, then this sling is folded double and held in the middle by a loop made for this purpose out of the same leather as the sling and of the same width.

Drum ring [*Barabannoe koltso*] — brass, about 1/8 inch thick and about 7/8 inch across, fixed to a small white or black (depending on the color of the accouterments) strap, the end of which is fitted between the shell and the top hoop, so that the ring lies on the shell and is next to the right side of the drum sling. This ring goes on the hook of the drummer's sword-belt. (Illus. 68.)

b.) **Fife case** [*fleitnyi futlyar*] for Caucasus troops — a case made of yellow brass, shaped like a flattened cylinder, 7 inches long without the cover and 7 7/8 inches long with it, with end about 2 5/8 inches wide in their longer aspect and about 1 3/4 inches in the shorter. The edges of the rims of both ends and of the lower edge of the cover are raised fillets. On the smooth front face of the case — 1/2 inch from the lower edge of the cover and equidistant from both sides — a round plate is soldered, made of the same brass, embossed with the coat of arms, 2 5/8 inches in diameter with an edge that also is raised and rounded. On the opposite face of the case, 1/4 inch below the edge of the cover, and on the cover itself 1/2 inch from the upper end of the case, are soldered and riveted [*c zaklepom naskvoz*] small, flat, oblong, ear-like brackets [*ushki*] made from thick brass wire, projecting 1/4 inch from the back of the case and a little over 1 3/4 inches wide. Inside the case is a piece of wood of the same dimensions as the case, with two hollow spaces into which fit the separated parts of the fife. The case is carried on a Russian leather strap, waxed and blackened, one end of which is turned back and sewn together to form a loop that goes around the waistbelt. The other end is put through the brackets of the case and likewise turned back underneath to fasten to a leather button sewn on the top loop. This strap is 1 3/4 inches wide and freely fits through the brackets. Its length must be about 19 1/4 inches so that when it is buttoned up it is as long as the frog for the sword [*tesak*]. This strap is also fastened below to a button on the frog by means of a special black, leather loop fitted around it between the brackets of the case. The cover, when taken off the case, must move freely up along the strap on its bracket so that the fife can be put into the case. (Illus. 69 and 70.)

c.) **Water flask** [*vodonosnaya flyaga*] — on the convex face of the water flask, right at the bend of the bottom end and equidistant from both sides, a small, flat, iron bracket is soldered and riveted, spaced about 1/4 inch from the face and about 1 1/3 inches wide. On the sides above are two iron knobs: one — right on the weld of the flask, and the other — on the opposite side. The heads of both are a little below the top end of the flask. The bases of the knobs must be about 1/3 inch high and not less than 1/4 inch across, for strength; the heads, though, are about 5/8 inch across. On the cap of the flask, instead of the tin bracket that used to be on top, an oblong bracket is soldered on the side right on the weld, made from thick wire, similar to the handles of a tea cup, and only so wide that when the cap is on the flask it does not project beyond the flask's back face.

Flask strap [*Flyazhnyi remen*] — 7/8 inch wide and 18 3/8 inches long. Its ends are rounded, and about 5/8 inch from the lower edge somewhat long slits are cut, rounded at the bottom, of the right size to button onto the knobs on the sides of the flask. For greater strength, these ends are reinforced for about 1 3/4 inches with additional leather, stitched around the slit and along the edges. The previous strap for the flask cap is replaced by a small strap 1/2 inch wide. One end of this strap is folded and sewn underneath itself to form a loop through which the large flask strap can freely pass. About 1/2 inch from its other end a long slit is cut for fastening to a leather button sewn on lower down. The strap is about 11 3/8 inches long from the top of the folded-back loop to the other end. The cap and its narrow strap are put on the flask so that the bracket is in back, and the end of the strap with the cut slit is passed through this bracket, then fastened to the button. The loop of the small strap's other end has the large flask strap put through it, and the large strap's ends are buttoned to the flask's side knobs. The strap on the knapsack's cover for holding the flask is sewn on lower down than previously, about 3 1/2 inches from the cover's lower edge. To fasten the flask to the knapsack, the former's large strap is put through the small loop on top of the knapsack cover and held by the strap on the cover, which strap goes through the lower bracket of the flask and then the lower small loop of the knapsack cover to fasten, as previously, to the middle buckle. Both straps lie under the flask when it is held in this way. When the flask is taken off, then the large strap can serve as a handle to carry it, just as before. The flask straps, black for all infantry, may be made from the current ones. (Illus. 71.)

d.) **Greatcoat straps** [*Shinelnye remni*] — the greatcoat straps, also for all infantry, are cleaned with black wax. However, they are of the same form as previously.

e.) **Sword-belt and crossbelt** [*portupeya i perevyaz'*] — the fitting of the sword-belt and cartridge-pouch crossbelt as presently approved by HIGHEST authority only differs from previously in that neither the sword-belt nor the crossbelt have any kind of bend at the ends, and in that there is not any small cross-strap [*poperechnyi trinchik*] connecting the crossbelt with the sword-belt that would prevent moving the cartridge pouch to the side to more easily take out rounds during battle. In the middle, where they go under the soldier's shoulder strap, both the sword-belt and the crossbelt retain a slight curve, as before, as much as necessitated by a man's build so that they do not protrude toward the neck but lie on the shoulders with their entire width and not on one edge.

f.) **Cover for the nipple of percussion weapons** [*Chekhol na sterzhen dlya udarnykh ruzhei*] — the nipple cover is of thick, shoe-sole leather, round and oblong, and must be large enough to not only cover the nipple but also the larger part of the nipple mount [*podsterzhink*]. Its upper diameter is the same as the diameter of the head of the cocking piece [*kurkovaya golovka*], while below it is a little bigger. On top of the cover there is still a round protrusion that closely fits the recess in the cocking piece; its lower edge is cut slanted. The cover has a small, black, Russian leather strap fitted to it, 1/4 inch wide by 4 3/8 inches long, the end of which has a buttonhole cut into it and a small button. This end, put through the lower swivel of the musket sling, on the gunlock side, is fastened with the small button. The interior of the cover is impregnated with grease and the exterior with black wax so as not to allow moisture to penetrate. This cover is to be kept over the nipple both in and out of formation (Illus. 72.) [(895)]

20 October 1851 - Approval is given to the following list and description of items that the soldier is to have in his **knapsack** while on the march or during inspections, and is applicable to all infantry troops:

a.) Items prescribed for both on the march and during inspections — two pairs of foot cloths [*portyanki* — cloth wrapped around the feet in place of socks, still used later in the 20th-century Soviet army — M.C.]; boots or boot materials; two shirts [*rubakhi*]; ear muffs [*naushniki*]; gloves with mittens [*rukavitsy c varizhkami*] (for summer); forage cap; tin box [*zhestyanka*] for percussion caps; drawing sticks [*peryshki*] with pointed ends; grease cloth [*zhirnaya sukonka*]; dry rag; screwdriver [*otvertka*], worm-hook [*pyzhovnik*], pointed cleaner [*zaostrennaya chistilka*] made of hard wood, all three in one thong; spare priming nipple [*zatravochnyi sterzhen*] tied with thread to a piece of glass [*steklyad*], smeared with grease, (if applicable).

b.) Items prescribed only for on the march — rusk [*sukhar*] and salt for four days; a pair of boot soles (if this is economical); a tin with polish or grease.

Gregory Chernetsov "Parade on Imparial field of S. Petersburg 6 October 1831

c.) Sundry items in the knapsack - button board [*pugovichnaya doshchechka*]; brushes: one each for clothes, boots, and whitening; chalk and paste; soap; scissors; dye for moustache; comb for dye; at least three needles; thread; thimble; awl; waxed end [*dratva*]; wax [*vosk*]; penknife; hair comb; small bag for stowing sundries [896].

26 January 1852 - Non-combatant lower ranks with **forage caps** of grey cloth are to have a cap band in the color of the collar of the regiment or arm to which they belong (Illus. 73) [897].

3 January 1853 - Non-combatant lower ranks with **frock coats** are to have these reach to the lower part of the knee [898].

18 February 1854 - The **saddles** of field-grade officers, and likewise regimental and battalion adjutants, are to have, in back, a valise [*chemodan*] of light-blue cloth, in the pattern prescribed for cavalry officers. A greatcoat, conforming to the regulation established for rolling cavalry troopers' greatcoats (*), is to be secured with small straps to the front arch above the saddle, in a leather case. This also applies to other infantry for the ranks mentioned (Illus. 74 and 75) [899].

29 April 1854 - Generals and field and company-grade officers of Grenadier regiments are to have, in wartime, **campaign greatcoats** [*pokhodnyya shineli*] of the same color and pattern as the lower ranks' greatcoats, with only the addition of pockets with flaps on the sides of the skirts (Illus. 76 and 77) and lace (in the same color as the buttons) on the shoulder straps:

a.) Generals — galloon as prescribed for the collar of a hussar general's *vengerka* [literally "Hungarian", a frock coat with hussar braid — M.C.], sewn completely over the entire width of the shoulder strap with the exception of a small space along the edges, as for the following ranks (Illus. 78).

b.) Field-grade officers — galloon as prescribed for cavalry sword-belts, sewn (a little bit away from the strap's edges) in three rows with two 1/4-inch strips showing in between (Illus. 78).

c.) Company-grade officers — the same galloon, sewn in two rows with a 1/4-inch center strip, and with the small rank stars established for epaulettes (Illus. 78).

Along with the introduction of these greatcoats, the following rules are established:

1.) For a better seating on horseback, all generals and field and company-grade officers who must be mounted when at the front of troops are to have the greatcoat skirts slit at the back, appropriate to stature, and fastened on the inside with buttons.

2.) Officers are not to wear the sash when wearing this greatcoat.

3.) The campaign sword-belt of the specially approved pattern is to be worn with the campaign greatcoat. These sword-belts are not only to be worn with the greatcoats and frock coats, but also with the dress coats [*mundiry*].

4.) Campaign sword-belts are to be worn only by company-grade infantry officers positioned in a frontal formation [*stoyashchii vo fronte*]; all infantry generals, field-grade officers, and regimental and battalion adjutants who are required to be mounted in a frontal formation [*vo fronte verkhom*] are not at all to use the campaign sword-belt, but when wearing the campaign greatcoat are to carry the half-saber on the ordinary sword-belt, worn under the greatcoat. For this a slit is to be cut lengthwise at the left pocket of the greatcoat.

5.) Officers ought not to wear officers' distinctions [*znaki*] with the campaign greatcoat, and they must wear knapsacks in all circumstances in which lower ranks are wearing theirs.

6.) When wearing the campaign greatcoat, officers ought not to wear any medals or decorations [*znaki otlichiya*] except for the Military Order of St. George, which must be worn in the manner prescribed for lower ranks.

7.) Warm collars [*teplye vorotniki*] are not to be sewn onto the campaign greatcoat, but they may be worn separately on top of the regular collar.

8.) During wartime, campaign greatcoats are to be begun being worn immediately upon setting out on campaign.

9.) In peacetime, greatcoats of the style and color now in use are to be worn [900].

17 June 1854 - The sixth replacement [*zapasnyi*] battalions are to have light-green piping around the top of the **forage cap** [901].

26 January 1855 - Lower ranks of the replacement battalions of Grenadier regiments are to have **sword-belts** and **short swords** [*tesaki*] along with the rest of their accouterments [902].

13 February 1855 - Approval is given to the following description of the new manner of fitting the **firing-cap pouch** [*kapsyulnaya sumochka*], applicable to Grenadier regiments and all other infantry troops:

The firing-cap pouch is fitted on the crossbelt as before, only a little lower on the right-hand side, and if a crossbelt is moved on the left shoulder so that the cartridge pouch comes to the right hip, then the left edge of this cap pouch must not come any closer than 1/2 inch to the knapsack belt over the right shoulder (Illus. 79) [903].

NOTES TO THE ILLUSTRATIONS
By Mark Conrad

1 and 2. Officers' epaulettes were gold with an embroidered cipher on a yellow field. Since 1814 lower ranks' shoulder straps were yellow with red showing through cut-out ciphers. In 1818 the shoulder straps were defined to be 2 1/4 inches wide with the 1 3/4-inch letter set 7/8 inch from the lower edge.

3. Grenadiers wore dark-green uniforms with red cuffs, cuff flaps, collar, turnbacks, and piping. Buttons, shako plates, chin-scales, scabbard mountings, buckles, bands on the musket barrel, and the trigger guard were brass. The musket sling was red. The shako and plume were black, cords were white. The greatcoat case was black and the flask was grey metal with a white strap. There was gold NCO lace on cuffs and collar with red showing on the outer edges. Here the NCO swordknot appears white with a long fringe, but another source shows the end ball to be mixed black, orange, and white with a short white fringe. The NCO plume has a white tip with an orange stripe, while the NCO pompon is white with a black hourglass shape. Not visible are the NCO's mixed black, orange, and white acorns and tassels on the right side of the shako, although the long cords down past the shoulder are plain white. Notice the small cord from the long shako cord to the shoulder-strap button, in use since 1825.

4. The dark-green coats are trimmed with white tape, each tape having a thin red stripe down the middle. A regulation of 1818 set the width of the tape as 7/8 inch. Since about 1820 the tape was placed closer together as shown here. In 1818 the base color of the swallow's-nest became red, and in 1825 the tape on the swallow's-nest was set in the diagonal position shown. Collar, cuffs, and turnbacks were otherwise as for other grenadiers. In 1825 all musicians were given NCO status and thus NCO lace on the cuffs and collar along with the NCO plume and pompon. This musician also wears the white pants with integral spats and white buttons. The drummer's fur apron appears to be brown, and the brass drum's dark-green triangles on the hoops point inwards with the top of the rim being all white. As confirmed in 1819, the drumsticks were straw colored in the first regiment of a division, black in the second, white in the third, and light green in the fourth.

5. Officers' gorgets were silver and gold, and which parts of the gorget were which metal was determined by rank according to a system prescribed in 1808. In the center of the silver pompon at the base of the black plume is the monarch's cipher (here H, being the Cyrillic N for Nicholas). The sash is silver with orange checks. The black bicorne has a black plume. The cockade is black and orange with a wide white edge, held in place with gold lace. Officers almost always wear white gloves.

6. In 1818 the grenadier regiments of the Separate Lithuania Corps were given white metal appointments instead of yellow, yellow cloth facings instead of red, and a yellow plastron.

7. Both figures have the white summer pants.

8. The base of the epaulettes appears to be a gold lace field.

12. Note the mixed black, orange, and white NCO tassels.

14. In this plate tiny grenades can be seen on the buttons. The NCO has grey pants, yellow shoulder straps, red cuffs, cuff flaps, and collar, and a dark-green forage cap with a red capband and red piping on the crown. The craftsman appears to have grey pants and jacket piped red, grey facings, yellow shoulder straps, and a grey forage cap piped red.

15. Yellow long-service chevrons were introduced in March 1825 on the basis of one for 10 years' service, two for 15, and three for 20.

17 The frock coat has a red collar and red piping on the dark-green cuffs. At the rear are two buttons at the waist and red-piped pockets.

18. White pants.

19. Black hilt bound with wire.

20. Dark-grey mittens are attached to the sword frog. The strap on the greatcoat case and the strap around the sides of the flask are white. All straps on the knapsack are black.

22. The white pants have a sharp side crease.

28 and 29. The metal heads of the entrenching tools are in black cases. The wooden handles are yellow in the first regiment of a division, black in the second, white in the third, and brown in the fourth. There is a small white strap connecting the ax handle to the crossbelt, just visible under the knapsack. Notice the tops of the turnbacks between the crossbelts. All four figures are wearing white pants.

30. Contemporary paintings and a color photograph of an actual sash show that all the checks are orange. The long tassels were silver on the outside hiding black and orange strands on the inside.

31. The lace detail at the top of the illustration is that of the small cross strap over the epaulette. The Cyrillic G stands for the Georgia Grenadier Regiment.

37. Cyrillic F for the Phanagoria Grenadier Regiment.

38. Cyrillic MR for the *Malorossiiskii* (Little Russia or Ukraine) Grenadier Regiment.

39. Cyrillic SG for Siberia Grenadier Regiment. The red silk mixed in the epaulette is not apparent in a black and white rendering.

40. From the center, the cockade is black, orange, black, orange, and white.

42. Collars for grenadier greatcoats are solid red. Shoulder straps are yellow. 47. The lockplate is stamped "TULA 1847".

48. All parts of the pouch are black.

52. The left-hand figure has white pants. Cuffs are dark green. Collar and piping are red. Rear pocket flaps are not piped. Shoulder straps are yellow. All equipment is black, including the strap around the lower part of the light-colored metal flask. The wool on the hat partially obscures the badge for distinction. Musket slings are still red.

56. Even the strap around the flask is black.

57. The pocket flaps at the rear of the skirt are not visible here.

59. Pants and coat, including collar and cuffs, appear to be grey with red piping. Shoulder straps are yellow. The forage cap is apparently grey with grey, not red, piping, but this is not definite.

61. All parts of the bugle including the badge are metal.

69. The case, including badge, is all metal.

71. The strap for the (empty) greatcoat case is now black. Straps on the flask and knapsack are black.

73. The uniform is all grey with red piping and yellow shoulder straps. The forage cap has a red capband but appears to have no piping.

74. The saddle girth has two large red stripes and three large dark-green ones. The shabrack is dark green with the gold galloon lace separated by red cloth. This is also true for the holster covers.

A note on colors: In Russian, "blue" [*sinii*] refers to dark blue while "light blue" [*svetlosinii*] means a lighter, somewhat brighter shade that English speakers would still not call sky blue (which in turn is translated as *goluboi* in Russian). Additionally, Russians can call for a very dark blue by saying *temnosinii*.

2.   MARINE AND INFANTRY REGIMENTS (*MORSKIE I PEKHOTNYE POLKI*).

11 February 1826 - The series of **uniform changes** issued on this date for Grenadier regiments are applied with equal force to Marine and Infantry regiments, with the only difference being that for the former the piping remains white (Illus. 80 and 81). The Infantry regiments of the Lithuania Corps (the Brest, Bialystok, Lithuania [*Litovskii*], Vilna, Volhynia, Minsk, Podolia, and Zhitomir) keep their present plastrons [*latskany*] and white appointments, while the pants [*pantalony*] receive yellow piping (Illus. 82) [904].

10 May 1826 - Generals, field-grade officers, and adjutants, when mounted in formation during the summer, are to wear white **pants** of either linen [*polotnyanyya*] or suede [*zamshevyya*] (Illus. 83) [905].

15 September 1826- Lower ranks who have completed the regulation number of years of faultless service and voluntarily remain on active duty are to wear a gold or silver**galloon chevron** [*nashivka iz galuna*] on the left sleeve, as described above for Grenadier regiments. [906].

1 January 1827 - Officers' epaulettes are to have little forged and stamped stars as **rank distinctions** in the same form and scheme as described above for Grenadier regiments [907].

31 July 1827 - Numbers and letters on the **covers** for shakos [*kivera*] and cartridge-pouches are to be painted in yellow oilpaint [908].

7 March 1828 - Lower ranks who return to their regiments from the Model Infantry Regiment [*Obraztsovyi Pekhotnyi polk*], as well as those who have previous service in Instructional Carabineer Regiments [*Uchebnye Karabinernye polki*], are to have tape [*bason*] on their **shoulder straps** in the same style and colors as described above for Grenadier regiments [909].

24 March 1828 - The **coats** of lower ranks are not to be tailored with cinches [910].

24 April 1828 - The **changes in uniform and equipment**, exactly as written above for Grenadier regiments, also apply with the only difference being that the shako plates for Marine and Infantry regiments have shields with cut-out numbers without grenades (Illus. 84, 85, and 86), and that all combatant ranks [*stroevye chiny*] of Musketeer companies [*Mushketerskiya roty*] and Marksmen platoons [*Strelkovye vzvody*] are given round **pompons** [*pompony*] for the shako as follows: officers — silver, lower ranks — woolen: Marksmen of the 1st battalion — yellow, Musketeers — white; Marksmen of the 2nd battalion — yellow with light blue, Musketeers — white with light blue; Marksmen of the 3rd battalion — yellow with green, Musketeers — white with green [911].

Shoulder straps and the field of officers' **epaulettes** remain as before with the number of the division and in the same colors: for the first regiment of each division — red, the second — white, the third — light blue, and the fourth — dark green with red piping. Only two regiments (the Prince Wilhelm and and Prince Carl of Prussia's) are left with ciphers on their shoulder straps and epaulettes instead of numbers.

The numbers for the **shako plates** are as follows: 1st Marine Regiment — *1*, 2nd Marines — *2*, 3rd Marines — *3*, 4th Marines — *4*, Prince Wilhelm of Prussia's — *5*, Prince Carl of Prussia's — *6*, Reval — *7*, Estonia [*Estlyandskii*] — *8*, Old Ingermanland [*Staroingermanlandskii*] — *9*, New Ingermanland [*Novoingermanlandskii*] — *10*, Field Marshal Kutuzov of Smolensk's — *11*, Velikie-Luki — *12*, Neva — *13*, Sofiya — *14*, Narva — *15*, Kopore — *16*, Belozersk — *17*, Olonets — *18*, Schlüsselburg — *19*, Ladoga — *20*, Archangel — *21*, Vologda — *22*, Kostroma — *23*, Galits — *24*, Murom — *25*, Nizhnii-Novgorod — *26*, Nizovsk — *27*, Simbirsk — *28*, Troitsk — *29*, Penza — *30*, Tambov — *31*, Saratov — *32*, Field Marshal the Duke of Wellington's — *33*, Mogilev — *34*, Vitebsk — *35*, Polotsk — *36*, Field Marshal Graf Dibich's — *37*, Poltava — *38*, Aleksopol — *39*, Kremenchug — *40*, Yelets — *41*, Sevsk — *42*, Bryansk — *43*, Orel — *44*, Kursk — *45*, Staroskolsk — *46*, Rylsk — *47*, Voronezh — *48*, Vladimir — *49*, Suzdal — *50*, Field Marshal Graf Saken's — *51*, Yaroslavl — *52*, Moscow — *53*, Butyrskii — *54*, Borodino — *55*, Tarutino — *56*, Ryazan — *57*, Ryazhsk — *58*, Belev — *59*, Tula — *60*, Vyatka — *61*, Kazan — *62*, Perm — *63*, Ufa — *64*, Yekaterinburg — *65*, Tobolsk — *66*, Tomsk — *67*, Kolyvan — *68*, Kamchatka — *69*, Okhotsk — *70*, Yakutsk — *71*, Selenga — *72*, Azov — *73*, Dnieper — *74*, Ukraine — *75*, Odessa — *76*, Crimea — *77*, Sevastopol — *78*, Kozlov — *79*, Nasheburg — *80*, Kura — *81*, Apsheron — *82*, Tiflis — *83*, Shirvan (later Field Marshal Graf Paskevich-Erivanskii's) — *84*, Tenginsk — *85*, Navaginsk — *86*, Kabarda — *87*, Mingrelia — *88*, Viborg — *89*, Petrovsk — *90*, Nyslott — *91*, Villmanstrand — *92*, Brest — *93*, Bialystok — *94*, Lithuania — *95*, Vilna — *96*, Volhynia — *97*, Minsk — *98*, Podolia — *99*, Zhitomir — *100*. The Infantry regiments Prince Wilhelm of Prussia's, Field Marshal Prince Kutuzov of Smolensk's, Narva, Simbirsk, Mogilev, Sevsk, Ryazan, Perm, Odessa, and Shirvan all have **badges for excellence** on their shakos [912].

18 May 1829 - Non-commissioned officers who have been recommended by higher command for promotion to officer rank by virtue of years of service are to have **silver sword knots** [913].

10 August 1829 - The Infantry regiments of the Separate Caucasus Corps and the attached 20th Infantry Division, being the Kura, Apsheron, Tiflis, Graf Paskevich's, Tenginsk, Navaginsk, Kabarda, Mingrelia, Crimea, Sevastopol, Kozlov, and Nasheburg, are to use **sheepskin headdress** [*shapka*] in place of the shako [*kiver*], of the same form as established for the Grenadier regiments of the corps (Illus. 87), and with a badge for distinction for Graf Paskevich's Infantry Regiment [914].

16 December 1829 - The red cuffs of officers' **frock coats** [*syurtuki*] are changed to dark green with red piping [915].

26 December 1829 - All combatant ranks are directed to have the **buttons** on their coats, frock coats, and greatcoats made with the raised image of the same numeral as on the shako plate [916].

20 February 1830 - The Kazan Infantry Regiment is to have the number *61* on the **shako plate and buttons**, for the Vyatka — *62*, Ufa — *63*, Perm — *64*, Selenga — *69*, Yakutsk — *70*, Okhotsk — *71*, and Kamchatka — *72* [917].

6 April 1830 - **Shako badges** with the inscription "*Za otlichie*" ["For excellence"] are awarded to the Infantry regiments: Schlüsselburg, Ladoga, Tambov, Vyatka, Tomsk, Kolyvan, Kamchatka, Okhotsk, Yakutsk, and Selenga [918].

20 August 1830 - Officers' rapiers [*shpagi*] are replaced with **half-sabers** [*polusabli*] of the same pattern as those received at this same time by officers of Grenadier regiments (Illus. 87) [919].

22 September 1830 - **Badges for excellence** are granted for the shakos of the Kabarda and Mingrelia Infantry Regiments [920].

9 May 1831 - The **Brest, Bialystok, Lithuania, Vilna, Volhynia, Minsk, Podolia, and Zhitomir Infantry Regiments**, which previously had plastrons and white appointments, are to have the same uniform as the other Infantry regiments. The newly formed regiments of the 26th Infantry Division have the following numbers: Modlin — 101, Praga — 102, Lublin — 103, Zamosc — 104 [921].

6 December 1831 - **Badges of distinction** with the inscription "*Za Varshavu 25 i 26 Avgusta 1831 goda*" ["For Warsaw 25 and 26 August of the year 1831"] are granted for the shakos of Infantry regiments: Prince Carl of Prussia's, Reval, Old Ingermanland, New Ingermanland, Velikie-Luki, Belozersk, Olonets, and Yelets (Illus. 88), while shako badges with the inscription "*Za otlichie*" are awarded to the Murom and Nizhnii-Novgorod Infantry Regiments [921].

31 December 1830 [sic] - A **badge for distinction** is granted for the shakos of the Chernigov Infantry Regiment [922].

1 January 1832 - Generals who have the **gold swords** decorated with diamonds and inscribed "*Za khrabost*" ["For courage"] are to wear them without sword knots [923].

8 June 1832 - Officers are permitted to wear **moustaches** [924].

3 January 1833 - Cloth half-gaiters [*polushtiblety*] are abolished for company-grade officers and lower ranks (Illus. 89). **Covers** for shakos and cartridge pouches, along with **sword knots**, are abolished for non-commissioned officers and privates. These sword knots are only to be retained by those non-commissioned officers who have them in silver [925].

20 January 1833 - **Covers** for shakos are restored as before [926].

28 January 1833 - Due to the reorganization of Army Infantry, Infantry regiments are to have the following **numbers** on their shakos and buttons: Neva (Neva Marines from 1833) — *1*, Sofiya (Sofiya Marines from 24 May 1833) — *2*, Prince Wilhelm of Prussia's — *3*, Prince Carl of Prussia's — *4*, Old Ingermanland — *5*, New Ingermanland — *6*, Belozersk — *7*, Olonets — *8*, Archangel — *9*, Vologda — *10*, Murom — *11*, Nizhnii-Novgorod — *12*, Field Marshal the Duke of Wellington's — *13*, Mogilev — *14*, Field Marshal Graf Dibich's — *15*, Poltava — *16*, Yelets — *17*, Sevsk — *18*, Vladimir — *19*, Suzdal — *20*, Moscow — *21*, Butyrskii — *22*, Ryazan — *23*, Ryazhsk — *24*, Yekaterinburg — *25*, Tobolsk — *26*, Selenga — *27*, Yakutsk — *28*, Azov — *29*, Dnieper — *30*, Brest — *31*, Bialystok — *32*, Volhynia — *33*, Minsk — *34*, Modlin — *35*, Praga — *36*, Viborg — *37*, Petrovsk — *38*.

After this reorganization **shako badges** with the inscription "*Za otlichie*" are to be worn by the following Infantry regiments: Prince Wilhelm of Prussia's, Archangel, Murom, Nizhnii-Novgorod, Mogilev, Graf Dibich of the Transbalkans', Sevsk, Ryazan, Selenga, Yakutsk, and Azov.

Prince Carl of Prussia's, Old Ingermanland, New Ingermanland, Belozersk, Olonets, and Yelets Infantry Regiments have **badges** with the inscription "*Za Varshavu 25 i 26 Avgusta 1831 goda*" [927].

20 February 1833 - All combatant ranks are given new pattern **summer pants** or **breeches** [*pantalony ili bryuki*], without buttons or integral spats (Illus. 90) [928].

22 February 1833 - Field and company-grade officers are not to use the hat, but rather wear the **shako** at all times. Regimental and battalion commanders, junior field-grade officers, and adjutants are permitted to have **riding horses** with long tails [929].

14 March 1833 - Due to the change in regimental organization, lower and upper **pompons** [*repeiki i pompony*] for Grenadier and Musketeer privates are to be in the following colors:

a) *Lower pompons.*
1st battalion: Grenadiers — red, Marksmen — yellow, Musketeers — white with a green center.
2nd battalion: Grenadiers — black with red below, Marksmen — black with yellow below, Musketeers — white with a black center.
3rd battalion: Grenadiers — red with light blue below, Marksmen — yellow with light blue below, Musketeers — light blue with a white center.
4th battalion: Grenadiers — light blue with red below, Marksmen — light blue with yellow below, Musketeers — white with a light—blue center.
5th battalion: Grenadiers — red with green below, Marksmen — yellow with green below, Musketeers — green with a white center.
6th battalion: Grenadiers — green with red below, Marksmen — green with yellow below, Musketeers — white with a green center.

b) *Upper pompons.*
1st battalion: Marksmen — yellow, Musketeers — white.
2nd battalion: Marksmen — black with yellow below, Musketeers — black with white below.
3rd battalion: Marksmen — yellow with light blue below, Musketeers — white with light blue below.
4th battalion: Marksmen — light blue with yellow below, Musketeers — light blue with white below.
5th battalion: Marksmen — yellow with green below, Musketeers — white with green below.
6th battalion: Marksmen — green with yellow below, Musketeers — green with white below [930].

5 May 1833 - Instead of being cut out, the numbers on the **shako plates** are to be made of tin (silver for officers) and fixed on the same small shields as for Grenadier regiments (Illus. 91) [931].

15 July 1833 - Upon the change in the organization of Infantry regiments, lower ranks are directed to have **forage caps** with piping in the following colors:

1st battalion: Grenadier platoon — upper and lower (above the band) piping red; Marksmen platoon — upper piping red, lower yellow; 1st, 2nd, and 3rd Musketeer companies — upper piping red.
2nd battalion: Grenadier platoon — upper piping yellow, lower red; Marksmen platoon — upper and lower piping yellow; 4th, 5th, and 6th Musketeer companies — upper piping yellow.
3rd battalion: Grenadier platoon — upper piping light green, lower red; Marksmen platoon — upper piping light green, lower yellow; 7th, 8th, and 9th Musketeer companies — upper piping light green.
4th battalion: Grenadier platoon — upper piping light blue, lower red; Marksmen platoon — upper piping light blue, lower yellow; 10th, 11th, and 12th Musketeer companies — upper piping light blue.
5th battalion: Grenadier platoon — upper piping white, lower red: Marksmen platoon — upper piping white, lower yellow; 13th, 14th, and 15th Musketeer companies — upper piping white.
6th battalion: Grenadier platoon — upper piping black, lower red; Marksmen platoon — upper piping black, lower yellow; 16th, 17th, and 18th Musketeer companies — upper piping black.
The crowns and cap bands of the forage caps, as well as the numbers on the band, are the same as for Grenadier regiments, except that for Marine regiments the cap band is dark green with white piping [932].

21 March 1834 - Upon the reorganization of the forces of the Separate Caucasus Corps, the Infantry regiments of this corps are to have **numbers** on the plates for their headdress [*shapka*] and on their buttons as follows: Tenginsk — 39, Navaginsk — 40, Apsheron — 41, General-Field Marshal the Prince of Warsaw Graf Paskevich of Erivan's — 42. Lower and upper **pompons** [*repeiki i pompony*] and **forage caps** are as for other Infantry regiments with the addition of pompons [*pompony*] for the headdress of Grenadier platoons: 1st battalion — red; 2nd — black with red; 3rd — black with light blue; 4th — light blue with red; 5th — red with green — identical with the pompons of 21 March 1834 and 4 April 1836 for the Georgia Grenadier Regiment [933].

26 September 1834 - Lower ranks are directed to wear the **knapsack** on two belts lying crosswise over the chest (Illus. 92) [934].

26 April 1835 - The following Infantry regiments are to have new **numbers** on their shako plates and buttons: Yekaterinburg — 19, Tobolsk — 20, Selenga — 21, Yakutsk — 22, Azov — 23, Dnieper — 24, Brest — 25, Bialystok — 26, Volhynia — 27,

Minsk — *28*, Modlin — *29*, Praga — *30*, Vladimir — *31*, Suzdal — *32*, Moscow — *33*, Butyrskii — *34*, Ryazan — *35*, Ryazhsk — *36* [935].

3 June 1835 - With the **21st Infantry Division** renumbered as the **19th**, the Apsheron Infantry Regiment is assigned the number *37* in place of *41*, and the Field Marshal the Prince of Warsaw's Infantry Regiment is assigned *38* in place of *42* [936].

20 August 1835 - The same directive regarding **knapsacks** [*rantsy*] is issued as described above for Grenadier regiments [937].

31 January 1836 - The lower ranks' **greatcoat** [*shinel*] is to have nine buttons instead of ten, as described above for Grenadier regiments [938].

27 April 1836 - The lower **pompons** [*repeiki*] are to be lined with black leather [939].

13 May 1836 - Girths for officers' **saddles** are to be dark green with red stripes [940].

21 October 1836 - Shako plumes [*kivernye sultany*] for Grenadiers are to be the same as established for Grenadier regiments at this time [941].

14 January 1837 - Handles of **entrenching tools** are to have the wooden parts varnished, and the same directives for the fitting and carrying of these tools apply as described above for Grenadier regiments [942].

15 July 1837 - Approval is given to the new pattern of officers' **sash**, identical to that described above for Grenadier regiments [943].

17 December 1837 - Approval is given to a new pattern of officers' **epaulettes**, identical to those introduced at this time for Grenadier regiments, i.e. with the addition of a fourth twist of braid [944].

17 January 1838 - The directive issued on this day concerning regimental **staff-hornists** applies with equal force to Marine and Infantry regiments [945].

4 January 1839 - Generals and field and company-grade officers are not to have any bows or bands on the front of their **pants** or **trousers**. These are to be worn completely plain in the manner prescribed for lower ranks [946].

16 March 1839 - Lower ranks' **pouch-belts** and **sword-belts** [*perevyazi i portupei*] are to be 2 3/5 inches wide, while **drummers' crossbelts** are as before, 4 2/5 inches wide [947].

25 July 1840 - The **Prince of Prussia's Infantry Regiment** [*Pekhotnyi Printsa Prusskago polk*], retitled from Prince Wilhelm of Prussia's Infantry Regiment [*Pekhotnyi Printsa Vilgelma Prusskago polk*], is to replace the letters P.W. on epaulettes and shoulder straps with the letters P.v.P. (Prinz von Preussen) (Illus. 94) [948].

16 October 1840 - The regulation concerning **gold chevrons** for lower ranks is confirmed as related above for Grenadier regiments [949].

25 January 1841 - The capes [*bolshie vorotniki*] of officers' **greatcoats** are to be 28 inches long as measured from the lower edge of the collar [*malyi vorotnik*] [950].

26 November 1842 - Until a new uniform is approved, officers and lower ranks of the Infantry regiments of the Separate Caucasus Corps are to wear **forage caps** in place of the sheepskin headdress [951].

8 April 1843 - A new pattern **shako** and **plume** are confirmed, identical with those approved at this time for Grenadier regiments (Illus. 95). Trim on the shoulder straps [*nashivki na plechevye pogony*] of sergeants [*feldfebeli*], distinguished officer candidates [*portupei-praporshchiki*], officer candidates [*podpraporshchiki*], non-commissioned officers [*unter-ofitsery*], and lance-corporals [*yefreitory*] is established following the same scheme as for Grenadier regiments, but being completely white without any red stripes for non-commissioned officers and lance-corporals [952].

8 April 1843 - A new pattern **epaulette for drum-majors** is approved, identical with that described above for Grenadier regiments [953].

10 May 1843 - The new shape and dimensions of covers for **cartridge-pouches** are approved, identical with those described above for Grenadier regiments [954].

2 June 1843 - The directives for fitting the **shako plate** and **badge for distinction** are confirmed, identical with those related above for Grenadier regiments [955].

2 January 1844 - Officers are to have a **cockade** on their forage cap as described above for Grenadier regiments [956].

8 January 1844 - **Staff-hornists** [*shtab-gornisty*], when mounted in formation, are permitted to have spurs [957].

9 May 1844 - Shakos are replaced by **helmets**, identical to those introduced for Grenadier regiments, but without plumes (Illus. 96) [958].

20 May 1844 - A new scheme for lower ranks' **forage caps** is approved, according to which the piping around the top is to be: 1st battalion — red, 2nd — white, 3rd — light blue, 4th — yellow, 5th — dark green, and 6th — light green. In Infantry regiments the cap band is as before — red, while in Marine regiments it is dark green with two white pipings, around both edges. On these, as on on other cap bands, there are numbers and letters cut out of yellow cloth for distinguishing companies, as before: for the first Grenadier company — Cyrillic *1. G. R.*, for the first Musketeer company — Cyrillic *1. R.*, and so on. For officers in all companies the cap band is the same as the lower ranks', but without numbers or letters, and the piping around the top is red [959].

7 December 1844 - Generals who are wearing a regimental coat when not on duty are to have a white plume [*sultan*] on the **hat** [*shlyapa*] instead of a black one [960].

4 January 1845 - Officers' **helmets** are to have, on the right side under the chin-scales, a cockade, as described above for Grenadier regiments (Illus. 97) [961].

16 December 1845 - Due to the change in divisional organization in the **Separate Caucasus Corps**, the Infantry regiments of this corps are assigned the following **numbers**: Tenginsk - 37, Navaginsk — 38, Apsheron — 39, Daghestan — 40, Field Marshal the Prince of Warsaw, Graf Paskevich of Erivan's — 41, and Samur — 42 [962].

21 January 1846 - Officers of **His Majesty the King of Naples' Infantry Regiment** (*Pekhotnyi Ego Velichestva Korolya Neapolitanskago polk*], (the former Neva Marine Regiment [*Nevskii Morskoi polk*]), are to have gold lace bars on the collars and cuffs of the coat (Illus. 98), and the entire regiment is to replace the number 1 on epaulettes and shoulder straps with the cipher of His Majesty King Ferdinand II, according to the specially approved design (Illus. 99) [963].

1 February 1846 - Officers of**His Majesty the King of Sardinia's Infantry Regiment** [*Pekhotnyi Ego Velichestva Korolya Sardinskago polk*], (the former Archangel Regiment), are to have gold lace bars on the collars and cuffs of the coat (Illus. 100), and the entire regiment is to wear the cipher of His Majesty King Carl Albert, according to the specially approved design (Illus. 101) [964].

2 February 1846 - His Majesty the King of Naples' and His Majesty the King of Sardinia's Infantry Regiments are to have black, horsehair **plumes** on their helmets (Illus. 98 and 100), while musicians, drummers, and hornists are to have red plumes [965].

23 June 1846 - Upon the introduction of percussion-lock weapons, the description for fitting the **firing-cap pouch** is approved as detailed above for Grenadier regiments (Illus. 102) [966].

9 January 1848 - On those days when they are obliged to remain in ceremonial dress (*prazdnichnaya forma*) after the mounting of the guard (*posle razvoda*), generals and field and company-grade officers are permitted to wear the **frock coat with helmet and plume** for walking-out [967].

18 April 1848 - On the occasion of **His Imperial Highness the Grand Duke VLADIMIR ALEKSANDROVICH** being named the honorary colonel (*shef*) of His Majesty the King of Sardinia's Infantry Regiment, with this regiment's name change to His Highness's Infantry Regiment, it is directed that:

a.) Officers and lower ranks of this regiment are not to have plumes on their helmets.

b.) Officers of this regiment are to keep the previous lace bars on the collars and cuffs of their coats. Their epaulettes, as well as the shoulder straps of lower ranks, are to be according to the specially approved design [968].(*)

* Although this order dictated that the epaulettes and shoulder straps of HIS IMPERIAL HIGHNESS THE GRAND DUKE VLADIMIR ALEKSANDROVICH'S Infantry Regiment be according to special design, i.e. with a monogram, this was not carried out, and in this regiment, on epaulettes as well as on shoulder straps, there is the numeral 5, i.e. the number of the division to which the regiment belongs.

8 August 1848 - Infantry regiments of the **Separate Caucasus Corps** receive the new uniform and equipment as confirmed at this time for Grenadier regiments and described in detail above under the paragraphs for 8 August 1848, 23 September 1848, 31 October 1848, 24 November 1848, and 25 November 1849 (Illus. 103 and 104) [969].

19 April 1849 - The fitting of belts to the newly introduced **English signal bugles** is approved as described in detail above for Grenadier regiments [970].

14 September 1849 - The **percussion pistol** model for officers is approved as described above for Grenadier regiments [971].

9 and 25 November 1849 - The fitting of **helmets** is confirmed as described in detail above for Grenadier regiments [972].

25 November 1849 - The directive about wearing the sheepskin **shapka** is confirmed as explained above for Grenadier regiments [973].

24 December 1849 - The grip on the hilt of the **gold half-saber** awarded for bravery is to be gold instead of wrapped in black, lacquered leather [974].

17 January 1851 - Approval is given to the descriptions for folding up and turning back the skirts of the **greatcoat** as laid out above for Grenadier regiments (Illus. 105) [975].

8 July 1851 - The **gun-lock covers** (*polunagalishcha*) are abolished and approval given to the patterns and descriptions of the **drum**, **fife case** for Caucasus troops, **water flask**, **greatcoat strap**, **sword-belt**, **crossbelt**, and **cover for the firing nipple** of percussion weapons, all as presented above for Grenadier regiments [976].

20 October 1851 - Approval is given to the list and description of items which the soldier is to carry in his **knapsack**, as presented in detail above for Grenadier regiments [977].

26 January 1852 - Non-combatant lower ranks with grey cloth **forage caps** are to have the cap band in the same color as the collar of the regiment or branch to which they belong [978].

[**7 April - 12 May 1852** - Regarding reworking **English signal bugles** to a uniform pattern. (RGVIA, f. 14940, op. 1-2 (*shtab 4-go Armeiskago korpusa 1830-64*), d. 407, 7 ll. 647 99-07) - M.C.]

3 January 1853 - Non-combatant lower ranks with **frock coats** are to have these reach to the lower part of the knee [979].

[**5-6 February 1853** - During reviews, the skirts of lower ranks' **greatcoats** must be buttoned up. (RGVIA, f. 14940, op. 1-2 (*shtab 4-go Armeiskago korpusa 1830-64*), d. 192, 2 ll.) - M.C.]

[**29 May 1853 - 4 February 1854** - Concerning the sewing of **boots** [*sapogi*] **from grey greatcoat cloth** for sick lower ranks in lazarets. (RGVIA, f. 14940, op. 1-2 (*shtab 4-go Armeiskago korpusa 1830-64*), d. 430, 32 ll.1365. 98-963.) - M.C.]

18 February 1854 - Field-grade officers, and likewise regimental and battalion adjutants, are directed to carry a valise and greatcoat on their **saddle** in accordance with the orders presented above for Grenadier regiments [980].

29 April 1854 - Generals and field and company-grade officers are to have campaign **greatcoats** in wartime, in the same pattern and worn according to the same directives as issued at this time for Grenadier regiments [981].

[**4 April 1854 - 21 November 1858** - Regarding changes in **officers' campaign uniforms**. (RGVIA, f. 14940, op. 1-2 (*shtab 4-go Armeiskago korpusa 1830-64*), d. 447, 41 ll. 1383. 98-891) - M.C.]

23 May 1854 - In the newly established seventh and eighth Replacement [*Zapasnye*] battalions only non-commissioned officers and musicians are to wear sword-belts. Other lower ranks only have the **crossbelt** for the cartridge-pouch but made in such a way that when the soldier must carry the bayonet alone without the pouch, then this crossbelt may be worn over the right shoulder. To this end the crossbelt is fitted with a sheath for the bayonet. Along with this the following description is approved concerning equipment for those troops for whom the sword belt is not authorized:

Crossbelt [*perevyaz*] — used for the cartridge pouch, also serving as a carrier for the bayonet, it has a sheath sewn on its left end of the same kind of leather as the crossbelt, 3 5/8 inches high and 3 5/8 inches wide. There is a leather button on the inside of this sheath. On the other end of the crossbelt the corners are trimmed just a little and a buttonhole is cut through here. Two straps, 8 3/4 inches long and 7/8 inches wide, are sewn to the inside of the crossbelt some 3 1/2 inches from the ends; these enable the crossbelt to be fastened to the pouch. Above these straps, at a distance equal to their length, two leather buttons are sewn; these fasten to the straps when the crossbelt is separated from the pouch. A small strap is also sewn on the left end of the crossbelt on the left side next to the sewn-on button;this is 2 5/8 inches long, 1 1/8 inches wide, and has a buttonhole slit down its middle for fastening the crossbelt with pouch to the coat [*mundir*], which is to say to the button at the waist of the coat. To turn this crossbelt into a sword-belt, it is unfastened from the pouch and put on over the right shoulder instead of the left, so that the end with the cut buttonhole goes into the sheath on the other end of the crossbelt and, hugging its edge, is fastened to the leather button that is sewn on the inside of the sheath.

Strap for attaching the fife case [*fleitnyi futlyar*] — cut out of the same leather as the sword-belt, 40 inches long and 1 1/2 inches wide. One end of the strap is rounded and has a leather button sewn here on its face, while the other end is trimmed to a sharp angle and has a buttonhole slit down its middle 7 inches from this pointed end. Some 18 1/2 inches from the pointed end of this same strap, a 5 1/4-inch seat [*posadka*] is made along its lower edge. Above this there is a movable loop of the same width as the strap, 14 inches long and with 2 1/4-inch, ear-like brackets [*ushka*] bent inward. By means of this strap the fife case is fastened to the short-sword and sword-belt, so that the tapered end goes from the left side of the case through the lower brass bracket, is put through the bracket on the movable loop and then through the upper brass bracket of the case, after which it is brought around to the right side of the case in the same place where the seat was made in the strap and put through the sword-belt opening that is above the frog. Going along the right side of the case exactly as on the left, it fastens at the very bottom of the case to the leather button sewn onto the other end of the strap. In order to fix the fife case to the short-sword, the latter is put into the movable loop on the strap, by means of which the case is attached to the sword-belt [982].

16 June 1854 - The seventh Replacement [*Zapasnye*] battalions are to have brown piping around the top of the **forage cap**, while the eighth battalions are to have turquoise piping [983].

13 February 1855 - The new method of fitting the **firing-cap pouch** is confirmed, as laid out above for Grenadier regiments [984].

[**22 May 1855 - 13 August 1855** - Regarding black accouterments and the **blackening of white deerskin accouterment**s. (RGVIA, f. 14940, op. 1-2 (*shtab 4-go Armeiskago korpusa 1830-64*), d. 747, 27 ll. 607 99-031) - M.C.]

NOTES TO THE ILLUSTRATIONS
By Mark Conrad

80. Dark-green uniform with red collar, cuff-flaps, cuffs, and turnbacks. Note that a thin strip of red cuff and collar shows above the NCO lace. NCOs have a white pompon with a black hourglass-shape. Swordknot colors are as in the Napoleonic Wars (see Viskovatov's Volume 10 or Osprey Men-at-Arms No. 185). By an order of 1818, Marine regiments had collar, cuffs, cuff-flaps, and turnbacks dark green piped white, and shoulder-straps as follows: 1st Regiment — red with the number 25, 2nd — white with a 25, 3rd — yellow with a 25, and 4th — dark green with red piping and a 28.

81. In 1818 musicians were prescribed plain white lace without any colored center strip, and the base of the swallow's nest was to be the same as the shoulder-strap (i.e., red, white, blue, or green according to the regiment's position in the division). Collar, cuffs, cuff-flaps, and turnbacks were red as for other infantrymen. Color schemes for pompons were unchanged from the Napoleonic Wars.

82. Colored plastrons were due to the Polish connection of the Lithuania Corps. Note the white pants with integral spats.

83. White summer pants. The saddle-cloth is dark green with a double lace border with a red stripe in between. The field of an officer's epaulette was the same color as lower ranks' shoulder-straps.

84. Note tent in the background.

87. Buttons on the overalls were white.

89. Officers' frock coats had red collars and red piping on the cuffs. The NCO's valise was black with a white strap. Knapsack straps were black but the strap on the canteen was white.

90. The officer's plume is black. Note (as in many of the other illustrations) that the black neckcloth is visible over the collar.

93. This plate is not referenced in the text but no doubt belongs to the entry for 20 August 1835.

95. Grenadiers had black plumes.

97. Visible here, as in other illustrations, is the stitching on the all-red collar.

103. All leather equipment, belts, and straps are black. The collar is red and the shoulder-straps are colored as for non-Caucasus infantry. Cuffs are dark green piped red. Skirt pockets are not piped in the infantry.

104. Again, red collar and dark-green cuffs piped red.

105. The greatcoat collar is red; shoulder-straps are as on the coat. Note that for infantry, greatcoat cuffs are not pointed.

NOTES

(813) Information from the Commissariat Department of the War Ministry.

(814) Ibid.

(815) Collection of Laws and Directives, 1826, Book I, pg. 105.

(816) Ibid., Book II, pg. 47.

(817) Ibid., 1826, Book III, pg. 255.

(818) Ibid., 1827, Book I, pg. 3.

(819) Ibid., Book III, pg. 89.

(820) Ibid., 1828, Book I, pg. 183.

(821) Ibid., pg. 211.

(822) Ibid., Book II, pp. 131 et seq.

(823) HIGHEST Order.

(824) Collection of Laws and Directives, 1829, Book II, pg. 221, § 12.

(825) Ibid., Book III, pg. 129, and information from the Commissariat Department of the War Ministry.

(826) Collection of Laws and Directives, 1829, Book IV, pg. 107.

(827) Ibid., pg. 115.

(828) Ibid., 1830, Book III, pg. 179.

(829) Ibid., 1831, Book II, pg. 39.

(830) Order of the Director of HIS IMPERIAL MAJESTY'S Main Staff, 1 January 1832, No 1.

(831) Collection of Laws and Directives, 1832, Book II, pg. 545.

(832) Ibid., 1833, Book I, pg. 419.

(833) Ibid., pg. 435.

(834) Ibid., pg. 11.

(835) Ibid., pg. 463.

(836) Ibid., pg. 465.

(837) Ibid., pg. 479.

(838) Papers from the Commissariat Department of the War Ministry.

(839) Collection of Laws and Directives, 1833, Book III, pp. 199-205.

(840) Ibid., 1834, Book I, pg. 199.

(841) Ibid., pg. 103.

(842) Ibid., Book II, pg. 89.

(843) Ibid., Book III, pg. 465.

(844) HIGHEST Order.

(845) Collection of Laws and Directives, 1835 Book III, pg. 171.

(846) Ibid., pg. 179.

(847) Ibid., 1836, Book I, pg. 137.

(848) Information from the Commissariat Department of the War Ministry.

(849) Collection of Laws and Directives, 1836, Book II, pg. 171.

(850) Ibid., pg. 209.

(851) Ibid., Book IV, pg. 157.

(852) Ibid., 1837, Book I, pg. 353.

(853) Ibid., Book III, pg. 47.

(854) Ibid., Book IV, pg. 325.

(855) Ibid., 1838, Book I, pg. 19.

(856) Information from the Commissariat Department of the War Ministry.

(857) Collection of Laws and Directives, 1839, Book I, pg. 3.

(858) Ibid., pg. 179.

(859) Ibid., Book III, pg. 83.

(860) Information from the Commissariat Department of the War Ministry.

(861) Order of the Minister of War, 9 September 1840, № 60.

(862) Ibid., 16 October 1840, № 71.

(863) Ibid., 23 January 1841, № 8.

(864) Archive of the Inspection Department of the War Ministry, papers for 1842, Section 2, 2nd Office, № 365.

(865) Orders of the Minister of War, 8 April 1843, №№ 46 and 47.

(866) Ibid.

(867) Order of the Minister of War, 8 April 1843, № 44.

(868) Ibid., 10 May 1843, № 63.

(869) Ibid., 2 June 1843, № 78.

(870) Ibid., 2 January 1844, № 1.

(871) Ibid., 8 January 1844, № 3.

(872) Ibid., 9 May 1844, №№ 63 and 64.

(873) Ibid., 20 May 1844, № 69.

(874) Ibid., 30 June 1844, № 81.

(875) Ibid., 17 November 1844, № 138.

(876) Ibid., 7 December 1844, № 147.

(877) Ibid., 4 January 1845, № 1.

(878) Ibid., 9 August 1845, № 101.

(879) Ibid., 26 April 1846, № 72.

(880) Ibid., 8 March 1847, № 46.

(881) Ibid., 9 January 1848, № 8.

(882) Ibid., 28 March 1848, № 66.

(883) Ibid., 8 August 1848, № 148.

(884) Ibid., 23 September 1848, № 163.

(885) Ibid., 31 October 1848, № 184.

(886) Ibid., 24 November 1848, № 197.

(887) Ibid., 14 March 1849, № 24.

(888) Ibid., 19 April 1849, № 31.

(889) Ibid., 14 September 1849, № 88.

(890) Ibid., 9 November 1849, № 110.

(891) Ibid., 25 November 1849, № 117.

(892) Ibid., 25 November 1849, № 118.

(893) Ibid., 24 December 1849, № 133.

(894) Ibid., 17 January 1851, № 7.

(895) Ibid., 13 December 1851, № 134.

(896) Ibid., 20 October 1851, № 120.

(897) Ibid., 26 January 1852, № 15.

(898) Ibid., 3 January 1853, № 3.

(899) Ibid., 18 February 1854, № 21.

(900) Ibid., 29 April 1854, № 53.

(901) Ibid., 16 June 1854, № 65.

(902) Ibid., 26 January 1855, № 18.

(903) Ibid., 13 February 1855, № 28.

(904) Collection of Laws and Directives, 1826, Book I, pg. 105.

(905) Ibid., Book II, pg. 47.

(906) Ibid., 1826, Book III, pg. 255.

(907) Ibid., 1827, Book I, pg. 3.

(908) Ibid., Book III, pg. 89.

(909) Ibid., 1828, Book I, pg. 183.

(910) Ibid., pg. 211.

(911) Ibid., pp. 131 et seq. [Sic, should be Book II? - M.C.]

(912) Collection of Laws and Directives, 1829, Book II, pg. 221, § 12.

(913) Ibid., Book III, pg. 129, and information from the Commissariat Department of the War Ministry.

(914) Collection of Laws and Directives, 1829, Book IV, pg. 107.

(915) Ibid., pg. 115.

(916) Papers from the Commissariat Department of the War Ministry.

(917) HIGHEST Order.

(918) Ibid., 1830, Book III, pg. 179.

(919) HIGHEST Order.

(920) HIGHEST Order directed to Field Marshal Graf Dibich of the Transbalkans, 31 December 1830.

(921) Ibid., 1831, Book II, pg. 39.

(922) HIGHEST Order.

(923) Collection of Laws and Directives, 1832, Book I, pg. 3.

(924) Ibid., Book II, pg. 545.

(925) Ibid., 1833, Book I, pg. 419.

(926) Ibid., pg. 435.

(927) Ibid., pp. 66-117, and list of badges for distinction, confirmed by HIGHEST Authority.

(928) Collection of Laws and Directives, 1833, Book I, pg. 463.

(929) Ibid., pg. 465.

(930) Ibid., pg. 479.

(931) Papers from the Commissariat Department of the War Ministry.

(932) Collection of Laws and Directives, 1833, Book III, pp. 199 et seq., and papers from the Commissariat Department of the War Ministry.

(933) Collection of Laws and Directives, 1834, Book I, pp. 102-118.

(934) Ibid., Book III, pg. 465.

(935) Ibid., 1835, Book II, pp. 43-46.

(936) Papers from the Commissariat Department of the War Ministry.

(937) Ibid., 1835, Book III, pg. 79.

(938) Ibid., 1836, Book I, pg. 137.

(939) Ibid., Book II, pg. 171.

(940) Ibid., pg. 209.

(941) Ibid., Book IV, pg. 157.

(942) Ibid., 1837, Book I, pg. 353.

(943) Ibid., Book III, pg. 47.

(944) Ibid., Book IV, pg. 325.

(945) Ibid., 1838, Book I, pg. 19.

(946) Ibid., 1839, Book I, pg. 3.

(947) Ibid., pg. 179.

(948) Papers from the Commissariat Department of the War Ministry.

(949) Order of the Minister, 16 October 1840, № 71.

(950) Ibid., 23 January 1841, № 8.

(951) Archive of the Inspection Department of the War Ministry, papers for 1842, Section 2, 2nd Office, № 365.

(952) Orders of the Minister of War, 8 April 1843, №№ 46 and 47.

(953) Order of the Minister of War, 8 April 1843, № 44.

(954) Ibid., 10 May 1843, № 63.

(955) Ibid., 2 June 1843, № 78.

(956) Ibid., 2 January 1844, № 1.

(957) Ibid., 8 January 1844, № 3.

(958) Ibid., 9 May 1844, №№ 63 and 64.

(959) Ibid., 20 May 1844, № 69.

(960) Ibid., 7 December 1844, № 147.

(961) Ibid., 4 January 1845, № 1.

(962) Ibid., 16 December 1843 [sic, should be 1845 - M.C.], № 151.

(963) Ibid., 21 January 1846, № 16.

(964) Ibid., 1 February 1846, № 24.

(965) Ibid., 2 February 1846, № 25.

(966) Ibid., 8 March 1847, № 46.

(967) Ibid., 9 January 1848, № 8.

(968) Ibid., 18 April 1848, № 77.

(969) Orders of the Minister of War: 8 August, 23 September, 31 October, and 24 November, 1848, for №№ 148, 163, 184, and 197, and 25 November 1849, № 118.

(970) Order of the Minister of War, 19 April, № 31.

(971) Ibid., 14 September 1849, № 88.

(972) Order of the War Ministry Director, 25 November 1849, № 117.

(973) Order of the Minister of War, 25 November 1849, № 118.

(974) Ibid., 24 December 1849, № 133.

(975) Ibid., 17 January 1851, № 7.

(976) Ibid., 13 December 1851, № 134.

(977) Ibid., 20 October 1851, № 120.

(978) Ibid., 26 January 1852, № 15.

(979) Ibid., 3 January 1853, № 3.

(980) Ibid., 18 February 1854, № 21.

(981) Ibid., 29 April 1854, № 53.

(982) Ibid., 23 May 1854, № 59.

(983) Ibid., 16 June 1854, № 65.

(984) Ibid., 13 February 1855, № 28.

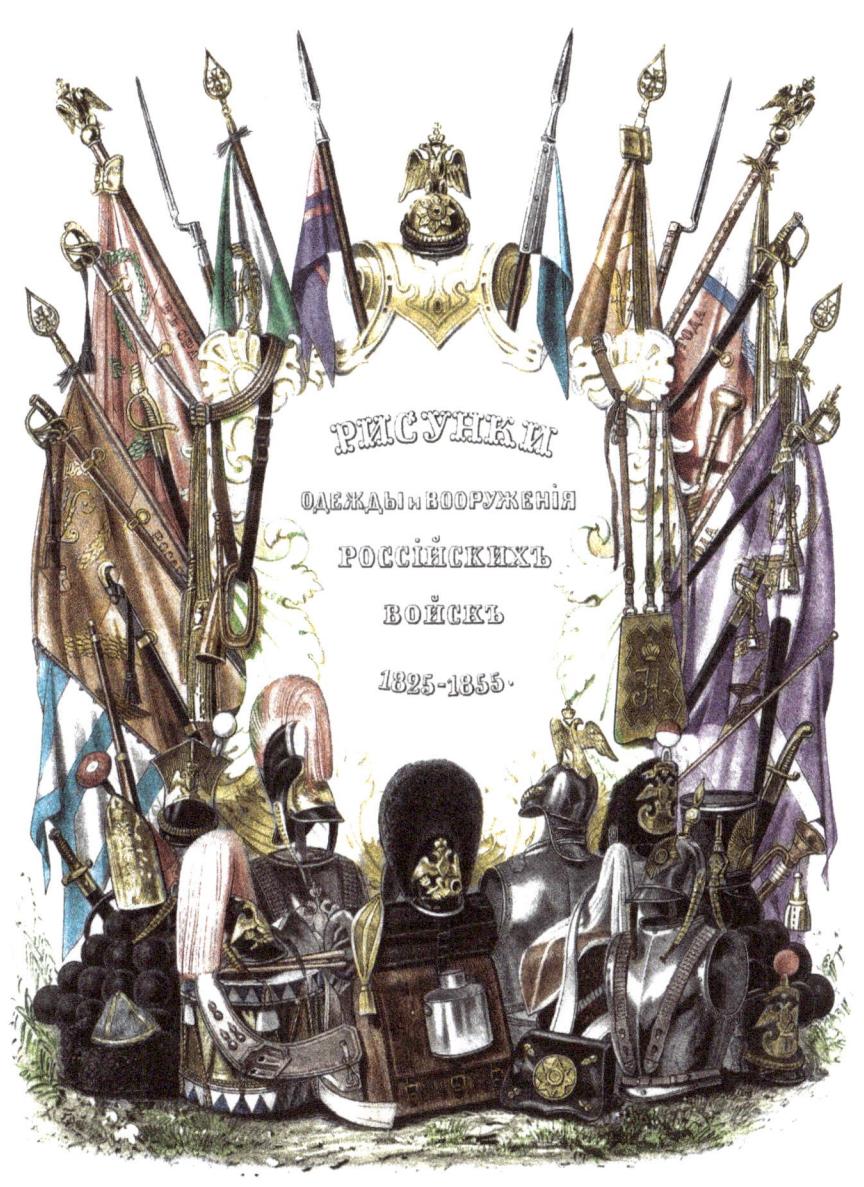

РИСУНКИ

ОДЕЖДЫ и ВООРУЖЕНІЯ

РОССІЙСКИХЪ

ВОЙСКЪ

1825-1855.

PLATES LIST OF ILLUSTRATIONS

1. Officer's Epaulette and Lower Rank's Shoulder Strap of His Royal Highness Prince Eugene of Württemberg's Grenadier Regiment, confirmed 21 December 1825.

2. Officer's Epaulette and Lower Rank's Shoulder Strap of Prince Paul of Mecklenburg's Grenadier Regiment, confirmed 11 January 1826.

3. Private and Non-commissioned Officer. Grenadier Regiments. 1826-1828.

4. Drummer and Musician. Grenadier Regiments. 1826-1828.

5. Company-grade Officers. Grenadier Regiments. 1826-1828.

6. Company-grade Officers. Samogitia and Lutsk Grenadier Regiments. 1826-1828.

7. Adjutant and Field-grade Officer. Grenadier Regiments. 1826-1828.

8. Officers' Epaulettes for Grenadier Regiments, with Rank Distinctions, established 1 January 1827. a) Ensign of the Kiev Regt. b) Sub-Lieutenant of the Yekanterinoslav Regt. c) Lieutenant of the Lutsk Regt. d) Staff-Captain of the Astrakhan Regt. e) Captain of the Kherson Regt.

9. Shoulder Straps for Grenadier Regiments, established 7 May 1828. a) Lower ranks returned from the Model Infantry Regiment. b) The same lower ranks who have previously served in Instructional Carabinier regiments.

10. Private and Non-commissioned Officer. Grenadier Regiments. 1828-1833. (In summer and in winter uniform.)

11. Company-grade Officer. Grenadier Regiments. 1828-1833. Note: In 1830 officers' rapiers were replaced with half-sabers as shown in illustrations 19 and 20.

12. Shakos, confirmed 24 April 1828.

13. Shako Plate for Grenadier Regiments and Badge for Distinction, confirmed 24 April 1828.

14. Non-combatant Non-commissioned Officer and Skilled Craftsman. Grenadier Regiments. 1828-1845.

15. Private and Company-grade Officer. Grenadier Regiments of the Caucasus Corps. 1829-1833. Note: In 1830 officers' rapiers were replaced with half-sabers as shown in illustrations 19 and 20.

16. Soldier's Shapka for Reg. of the Grenadier Brigade of the Separate Caucasus Corps, 10 August 1829.

17. Field-grade Officer. Grenadier Regiments. 1829-1844.

18. Field-grade Officer. Grenadier Regiments. 1830-1845. (In summer Sunday uniform.)

19. Infantry Officer's Half-saber, confirmed 20 August 1830.

20. Private and Non-commissioned Officer. Grenadier Regiments. 1833-1843.

21. Company-grade Officer. Grenadier Regiments. 1833-1843. (In everyday uniform.)

22. Company-grade Officer and Non-commissioned Officer. Grenadier Regiments. 1833-1843.

23. Shako Plate for Grenadier Regiments, confirmed 5 May 1833.

24. Officer's Epaulette and Lower Rank's Shoulder Strap of His Royal Highness the Hereditary Prince of Orange's Grenadier Regiment, confirmed 29 January 1834.

25. Private. Grenadier Regiments. 1835-1843.

26. Officer's Epaulette and Lower Rank's Shoulder Strap of Prince Frederick of the Netherlands' Grenadier Regiment, confirmed 14 June 1835.

27. Company-grade Officer. Grenadier Regiments. 1836-1843.

28. Privates. Grenadier Regiments. 1837-1843. (With entrenching tools.)

29. Privates. Grenadier Regiments. 1837-1843. (With entrenching tools.)

30. Officer's Sash, confirmed 15 July 1837.

31. Officer's Epaulette, confirmed 17 December 1837.

32. Officer's Epaulette and Rank's Shoulder Strap of Arch-Duke Francis Charles' Grenadier Reg., 16 August 1838.

33. Officer's Epaulette and Rank's Shoulder Strap of His Majesty the King of Prussia's Grenadier Reg., 26 May 1840.

34. Officer's Epaulette and Lower Rank's Shoulder Strap of his imperial highness the ereditary Tsesarevich's

Yekaterinoslav Grenadier Regiment.

35. Non-commissioned Officer and Company-grade Officer. Grenadier Regiments. 1839-1843.

36. Shakos, confirmed 8 April 1843.

37. Shoulder Straps for Grenadier Regiments, with Rank Distinctions, established 8 April 1843. a) Sergeants [*Feldfebeli*], b) Distinguished Officer Candidates [*Portupei Praporshchiki*], and c) Section Non-commissioned Officers [*Otdelnye Unter-Ofitsery*].

38. Shoulder Straps for Grenadier Regiments, with Rank Distinctions, established 8 April 1843. a) Junior Non-commissioned Officers [*Mladshie Unter-Ofitsery*] b) Lance-Corporals [*Yefreitory*].

39. Drum-major's Epaulette for Grenadier Regiments, confirmed 8 April 1843.

40. Officer's Forage Cap with Cockade, confirmed 2 January 1844.

41. Private and Non-commissioned Officer. Grenadier Regiments. 1844-1846.

42. Lower Ranks' Helmets for Grenadier Regiments, confirmed 9 May 1844.

43. Field-grade Officer. his imperial highness the ereditary Tsesarevich's Yekaterinoslav Grenadier Reg. 1844.

44. Company-grade Officer. Grenadier Regiments. 1844.

45. Officer's Epaulette and Lower Rank's Shoulder Strap of his imperial highness the Grand Duke Michael Pavolovich's Grenadier Regiment, confirmed 30 June 1844.

46. Company-grade Officer. Grenadier Reg. 1845-1854. (His Majesty the King of Prussia's, his imperial highness the ereditary Tsesarevich's , and his imperial highness the Grand Duke Michael Pavolovich's Regiments.)

47. Percussion Lock for Infantry Muskets, introduced in 1846.

48. Infantry Firing-cap Pouch, confirmed 23 June 1846.

49. Private. Grenadier Regiments. 1846-1849.

50. Company-grade Officer. Grenadier Regiments. 1848-1855.

51. Officer's Epaulette and Lower Rank's Shoulder Strap of his imperial highness Grand Duke Constantine Nikolaevich's Grenadier Regiment, confirmed 28 March 1848.

52. Privates. his imperial highness Grand Duke Constantine Nikolaevich's Grenadier Regiment. 1848-1855.

53. Non-commissioned Officer. his imperial highness the Grand Duke Constantine Nikolaevich's Grenadier Regiment. 1848-1855.

54. Waistbelt with Frog for Infantry Troops of the Separate Caucasus Corps, confirmed 8 August 1848.

55. Lower Rank's Ammunition Pouch for Infantry Troops of the Separate Caucasus Corps, confirmed 8 August 1848.

56. Lower Rank's Knapsack for Infantry Troops of the Separate Caucasus Corps, confirmed 8 August 1848.

57. Company-grade Officers. his imperial highness Grand Duke Constantine Nikolaevich's Grenadier Regiment. 1848-1855.

58. Officer's Half-saber with Sword-belt for Infantry Troops of the Separate Caucasus Corps, confirmed 8 August 1848.

59. Non-combatant. his imperial highness Grand Duke Constantine Nikolaevich'sGrenadier Reg. 1848-1855.

60. Officer's Epaulette and Lower Rank's Shoulder Strap of The King of the Netherlands' Grenadier Regiment, confirmed 14 March 1849.

61. Infantry Signal Bugle (English Pattern), confirmed 19 April 1849.

62. Bugler. Grenadier Regiments. 1849-1855.

63. Infantry Officer's Percussion Pistol, confirmed 14 September 1849.

64. Lower Rank's Helmet for Grenadier Regiments, confirmed 9 and 25 November 1849.

65. Infantry Officer's Gold Half-saber "For Courage", confirmed 24 December 1849.

66. Non-commissioned Officer. Grenadier Regiments. 1851-1855.

67. Private. Grenadier Regiments. 1851-1854.

68. Infantry Drum, confirmed 8 July 1851.

69. Fife Case for Infantry Troops of the Separate Caucasus Corps, confirmed 8 July 1851.

70. Fifer. His imperial highness the Grand duke Contantine Nikolaevich's Grenadier Regiment. 1851-1855.

71. Infantry Water Flask and Greatcoat Strap, confirmed July 8th 1851.

72. Firing-Nipple Cover for Percussion Infantry Muskets, confirmed 8 July 1851.

73. Non-combatant. Grenadier Regiments. 1852-1855.

74. Infantry Officer's Horse Furniture, confirmed 18 February 1854.

75. Field-grade Officer. Grenadier Regiments. 1854 and 1855.

76. Company-grade Officer. Grenadier Regiments. 1854 and 1855.

77. Company-grade Officer. Grenadier Regiments. 1854 and 1855.

78. Campaign Greatcoat Shoulder Straps for Grenadier Regiments, established April 29th 1854. a) General, b) Field-grade Officer, and c) Company-grade Officer.

79. Private. Grenadier Regiments. 1855.

80. Non-commissioned Officers. Musketeer Companies of Infantry and Marine Regiments. 1826-1828.

81. Drummer. Musketeer Companies of Infantry Regiments. 1826-1828.

82. Company-grade Officers. Infantry Regiments of the Lithuania Corps. 1826-1828.

83. Field-grade Officer and Adjutant. Infantry and Marine Regiments. 1826-1828.

84. Private. Infantry Regiment. 1828-1830.

85. Company-grade Officer. Grenadier Companies of Infantry Regiments. 1826-1833.

86. Shako Plate for Infantry Regiments, confirmed 24 April 1828.

87. Company-grade Officer. Infantry Regiments of the Caucasus Corps. 1830-1834.

88. Shako Badge for Distinction with the Inscription: "For Warsaw 25 and 26 August of the year 1831", confirmed December 6th 1831.

89. Company-grade Officer and Non-commissioned Officer. Infantry Regiments. 1833-1835.

90. Company-grade Officer and Private. Marine Regiments. 1833-1846.

91. Shako Plate for Infantry Regiments, confirmed 5 May 1833.

92. Private. Infantry Regiments. 1835-1843.

93. Company-grade Officer. Musketeer Companies of Infantry Regiments. 1835-1843.

94. Officer's Epaulette and Lower Rank's Shoulder Strap for The Prince of Prussia's Infantry Regiment, confirmed 25 July 1840.

95. Grenadier. Infantry Regiments. 1843 and 1844.

96. Non-commissioned Officer and Company-grade Officer. Infantry Regiments. 1844-1846.

97. Field-grade Officer. Infantry Regiments. 1845-1849.

98. Field-grade Officer. His Majesty the King of Naples' Infantry Regiment. 1846-1849.

99. Officer's Epaulette and Lower Rank's Shoulder Strap of His Majesty the King of Naples' Infantry Regiment, confirmed 21 January 1846.

100. Company-grade Officer. His Majesty the King of Sardinia's Infantry Regiment. 1846-1848. Note: In 1848 this regiment became His Imperial Highness the Grand Duke Vladimir Aleksandrovich's Infantry Regiment.

101. Officer's Epaulette and Lower Rank's Shoulder Strap of His Majesty the King of Sardinia's Infantry Regiment, confirmed 1 February 1846.

102. Private. His Majesty the King of Naples' Infantry Regiment. 1846-1849.

103. Privates. Infantry Regiments of the Separate Caucasus Corps. 1848-1855.

104. Field-grade Officer. Infantry Regiments of the Separate Caucasus Corps. 1848-1855.

105. Drummer. Infantry Regiments. 1851-1855.

Private and Non-commissioned Officer. Grenadier Regiments. 1826-1828

Drummer and Musician. Grenadier Regiments. 1826-1828

Officer's Epaulette and Lower Rank's Shoulder Strap of His Royal Highness Prince Eugene of Württemberg's Grenadier Regiment, confirmed 21 December 1825.

. Officer's Epaulette and Lower Rank's Shoulder Strap of Prince Paul of Mecklenburg's Grenadier Regiment, confirmed 11 January 1826

Company-grade Officers. Grenadier Regiments. 1826-1828

Company-grade Officers. Samogitia and Lutsk Grenadier Regiments. 1826-1828

Adjutant and Field-grade Officer. Grenadier Regiments. 1826-1828

Officers' Epaulettes for Grenadier Regiments, with Rank Distinctions, established 1 January 1827. a) Ensign of the Kiev Regt. b) Sub-Lieutenant of the Yekanterinoslav Regt. c) Lieutenant of the Lutsk Regt. d) Staff-Captain of the Astrakhan Regt. e) Captain of the Kherson Regt

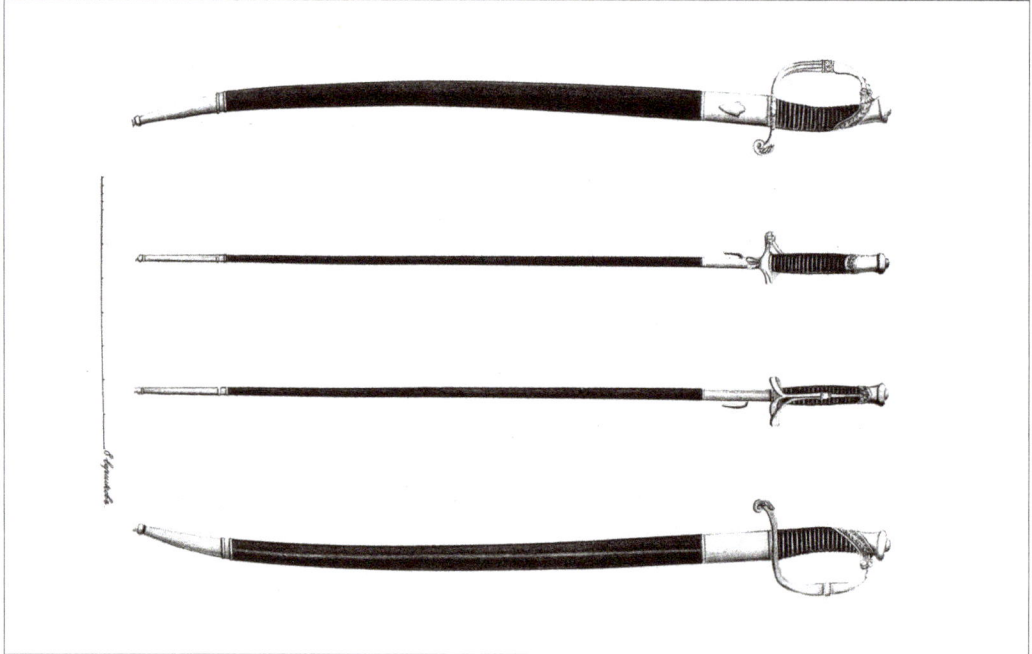

Shoulder Straps for Grenadier Regiments, established 7 May 1828. a) Lower ranks returned from the Model Infantry Regiment. b) The same lower ranks who have previously served in Instructional Carabinier regiments

Infantry Officer's Half-saber, confirmed 20 August 1830

Private and Non-commissioned Officer. Grenadier Regiments. 1828-1833. (In summer and in winter uniform.)

Company-grade Officer. Grenadier Regiments. 1828-1833. Note: In 1830 officers' rapiers were replaced with half-sabers as shown in illustrations 19 and 20

Shakos, confirmed 24 April 1828

Shako Plate for Grenadier Regiments and Badge for Distinction, confirmed 24 April 1828

Non-combatant Non-commissioned Officer and Skilled Craftsman. Grenadier Regiments. 1828-1845

Private and Company-grade Officer. Grenadier Regiments of the Caucasus Corps. 1829-1833. Note: In 1830 officers' rapiers were replaced with half-sabers as shown in illustrations 19 and 20.

Soldier's Shapka for Regiments of the Grenadier Brigade of the Separate Caucasus Corps, confirmed 10 August 1829

Field-grade Officer. Grenadier Regiments. 1829-1844.

Field-grade Officer. Grenadier Regiments. 1830 1845. (In summer Sunday uniform.)

Private and Non-commissioned Officer. Grenadier Regiments. 1833-1843

Company-grade Officer. Grenadier Regiments. 1833-1843. (In everyday uniform.)

Company-grade Officer and Non-commissioned Officer. Grenadier Regiments. 1833-1843

Shako Plate for Grenadier Regiments, confirmed 5 May 1833

Shako Plate for Grenadier Regiments, confirmed 5 May 1833

Officer's Epaulette and Lower Rank's Shoulder Strap of His Royal Highness the Hereditary Prince of Orange's Grenadier Reg. confirmed 29 January 1834

Officer's Epaulette and Lower Rank's Shoulder Strap of Prince Frederick of the Netherlands' Grenadier Regiment, confirmed 14 June 1835

Company-grade Officer. Grenadier Regiments. 1836-1843

Privates. Grenadier Regiments. 1837-1843. (With entrenching tools.)

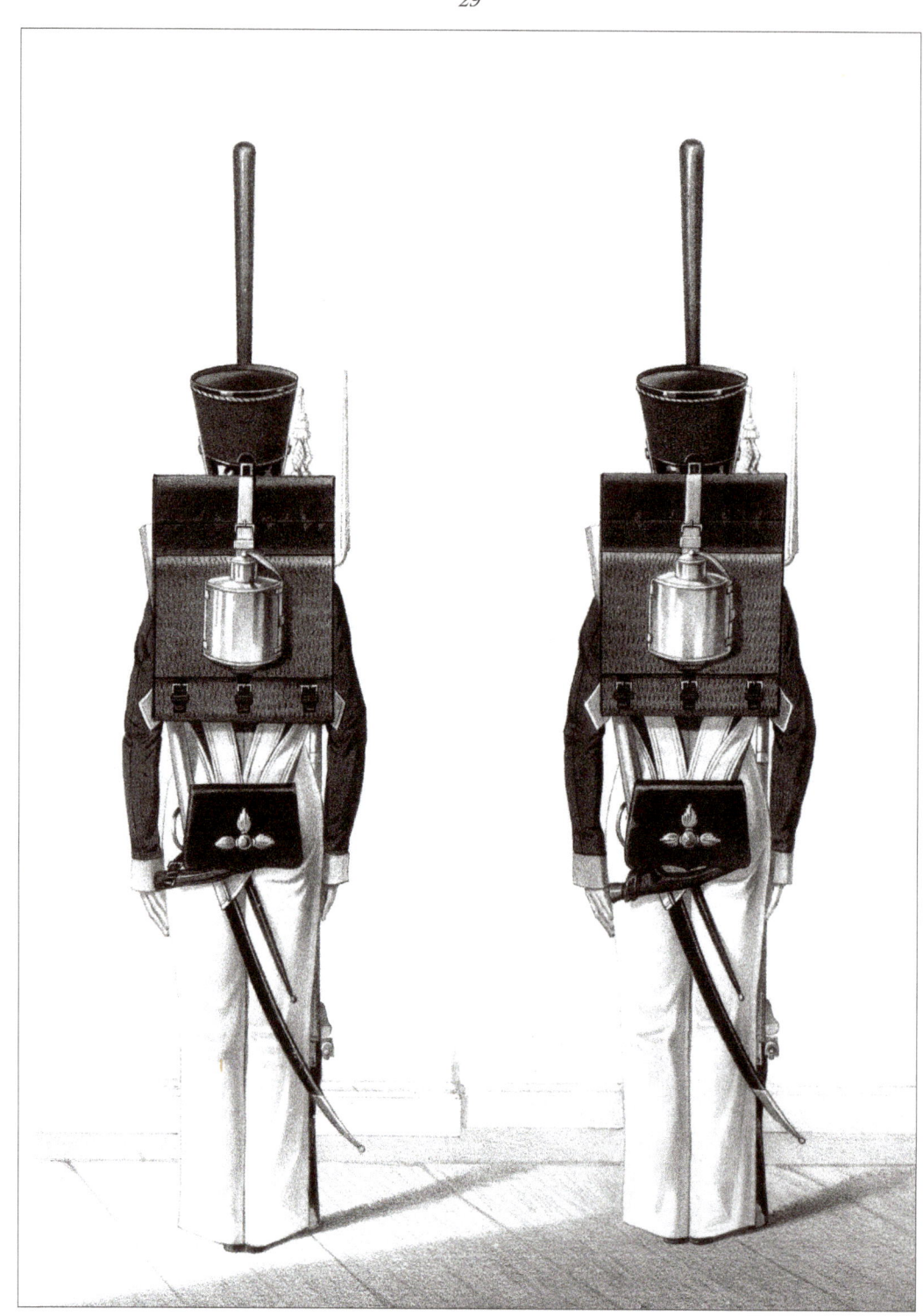

Privates. Grenadier Regiments. 1837-1843. (With entrenching tools.)

Officer's Sash, confirmed 15 July 1837

Officer's Epaulette, confirmed 17 December 1837

32 - 33 .34

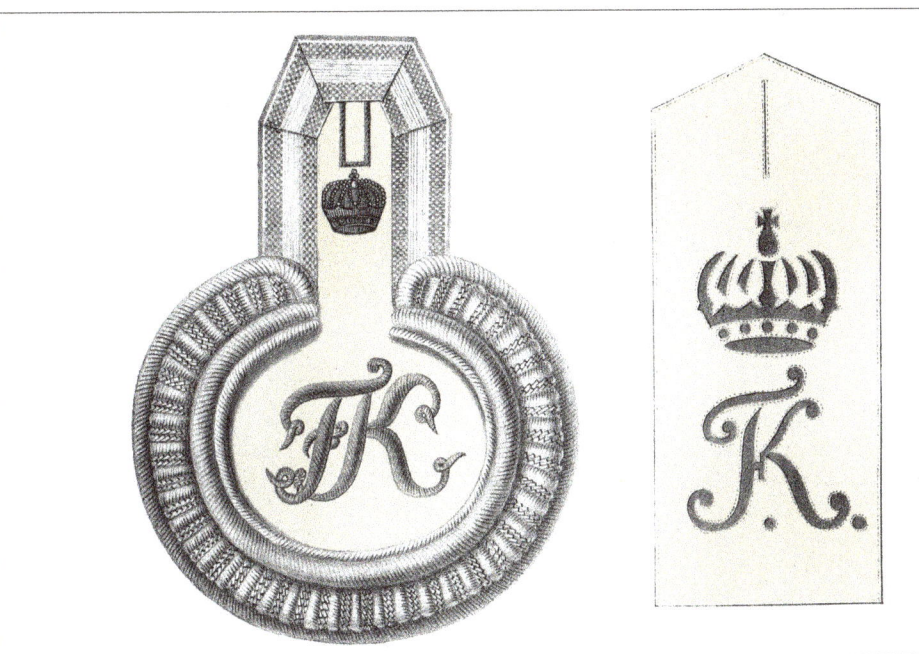

Officer's Epaulette and Lower Rank's Shoulder Strap of Arch-Duke Francis Charles' Grenadier Regiment, confirmed 16 August 1838
Officer's Epaulette and Lower Rank's Shoulder Strap of His Majesty the King of Prussia's Grenadier Regiment, confirmed 26 May 1840.
Officer's Epaulette and Lower Rank's Shoulder Strap of his imperial Yekaterinoslav Grenadier Regiment.

Non-commissioned Officer and Company-grade Officer. Grenadier Regiments. 1839-1843

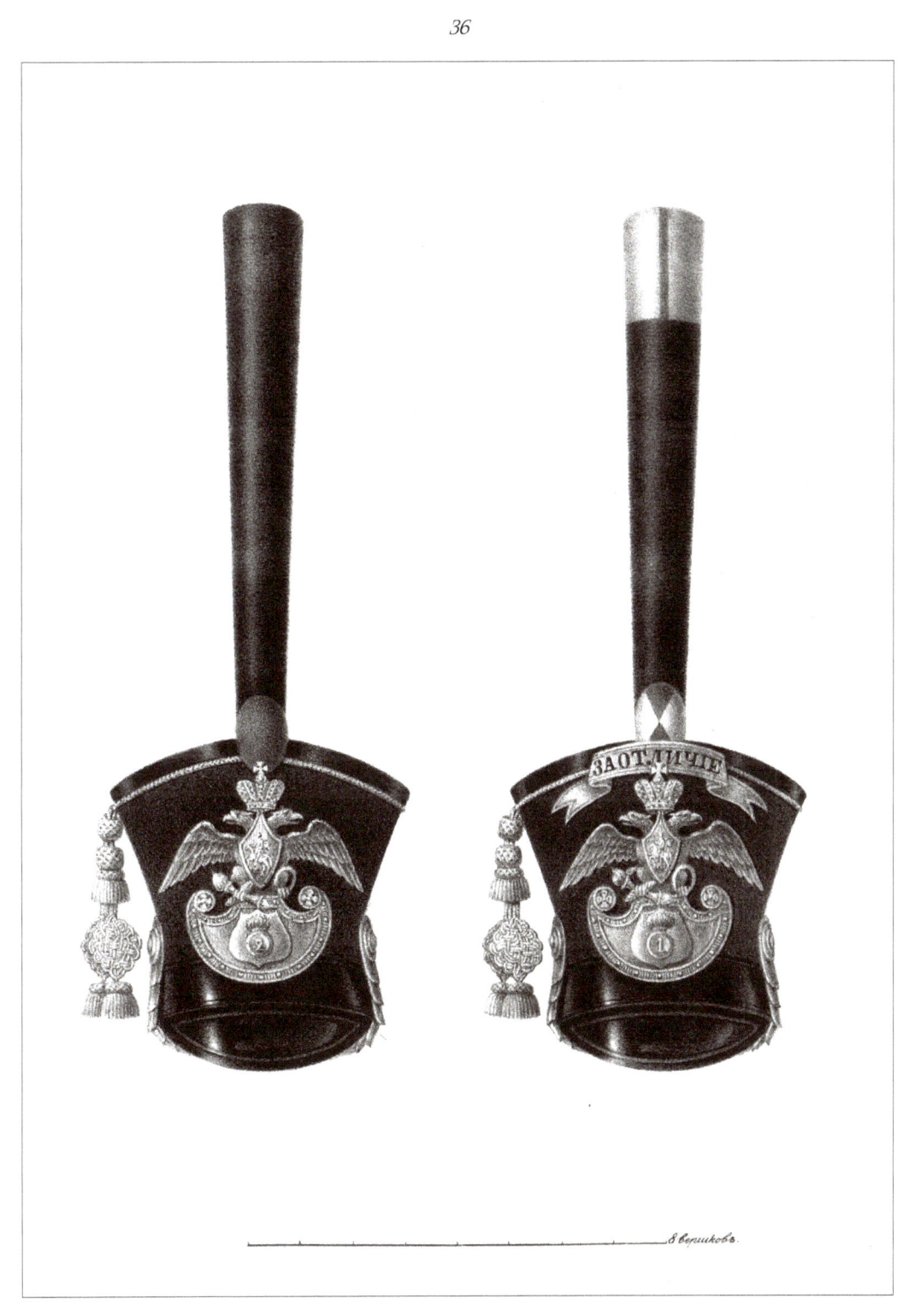

Shakos, confirmed 8 April 1843

Shoulder Straps for Grenadier Regiments, with Rank Distinctions, established 8 April 1843. a) Sergeants [Feldfebeli], b) Distinguished Officer Candidates and c) Section Non-commissioned Officers

Shoulder Straps for Grenadier Regiments, with Rank Distinctions, established 8 April 1843. a) Junior Non-commissioned Officers b) Lance-Corporals

Drum-major's Epaulette for Grenadier Regiments, confirmed 8 April 1843

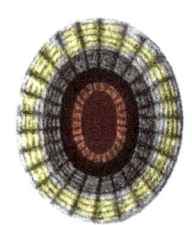

4 вершка.

Officer's Forage Cap with Cockade, confirmed 2 January 1844

Private and Non-commissioned Officer. Grenadier Regiments. 1844-1846

Lower Ranks' Helmets for Grenadier Regiments, confirmed 9 May 1844

Field-grade Officer. His imperial Yekaterinoslav Grenadier Regiment. 1844

Company-grade Officer. Grenadier Regiments. 1844

Officer's Epaulette and Lower Rank's Shoulder Strap of his imperial Grenadier Regiment, confirmed 30 June 1844

Officer's Epaulette and Lower Rank's Shoulder Strap of his imperial Grenadier Regiment, confirmed 28 March 1848

Officer's Epaulette and Lower Rank's Shoulder Strap of The King of the Netherlands' Grenadier Regiment, confirmed 14 March 1849

Company-grade Officer. Grenadier Regiments. 1845-1854. (His Majesty the King of Prussia's, his imperial Regiments.)

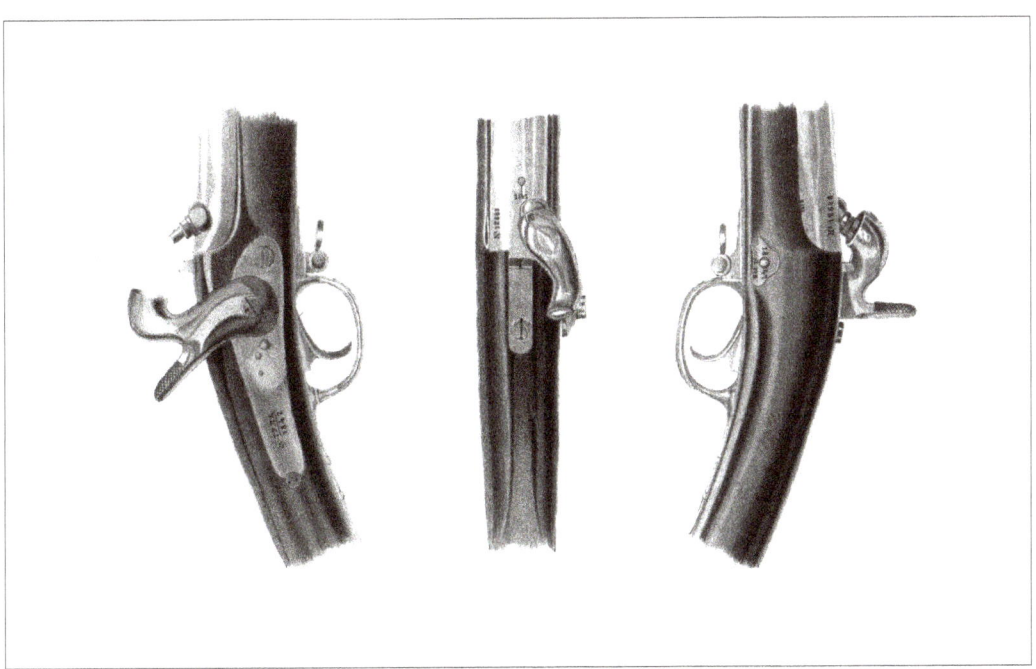

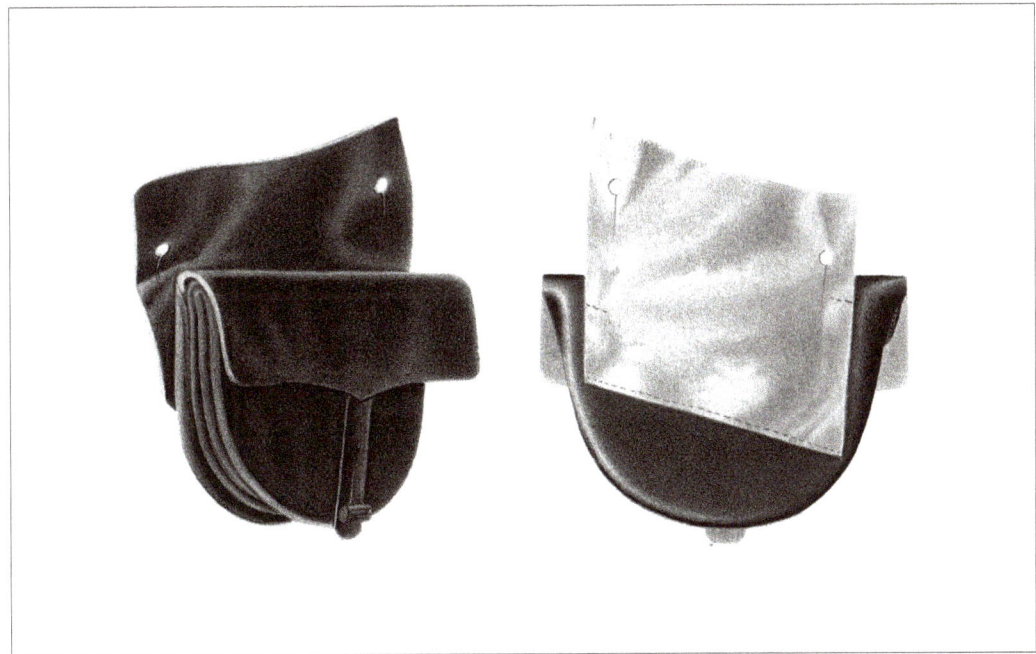

Percussion Lock for Infantry Muskets, introduced in 1846 - Infantry Firing-cap Pouch, confirmed 23 June 1846

Private. Grenadier Regiments. 1846-1849

Company-grade Officer. Grenadier Regiments. 1848-1855

Privates. His imperial Grenadier Regiment. 1848-1855

Non-commissioned Officer. his imperial Grenadier Regiment. 1848-1855

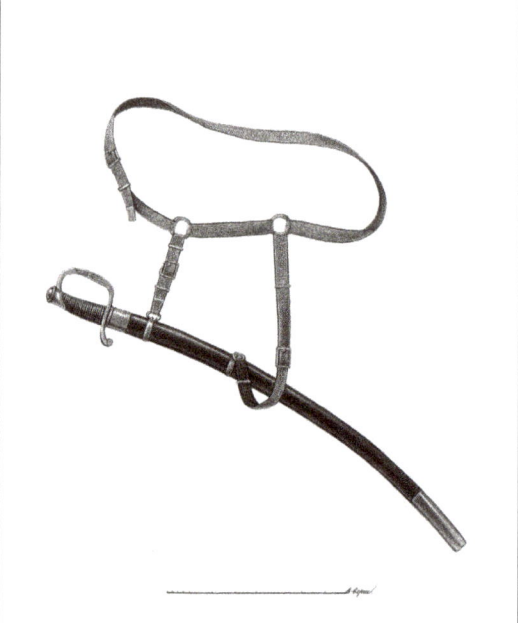

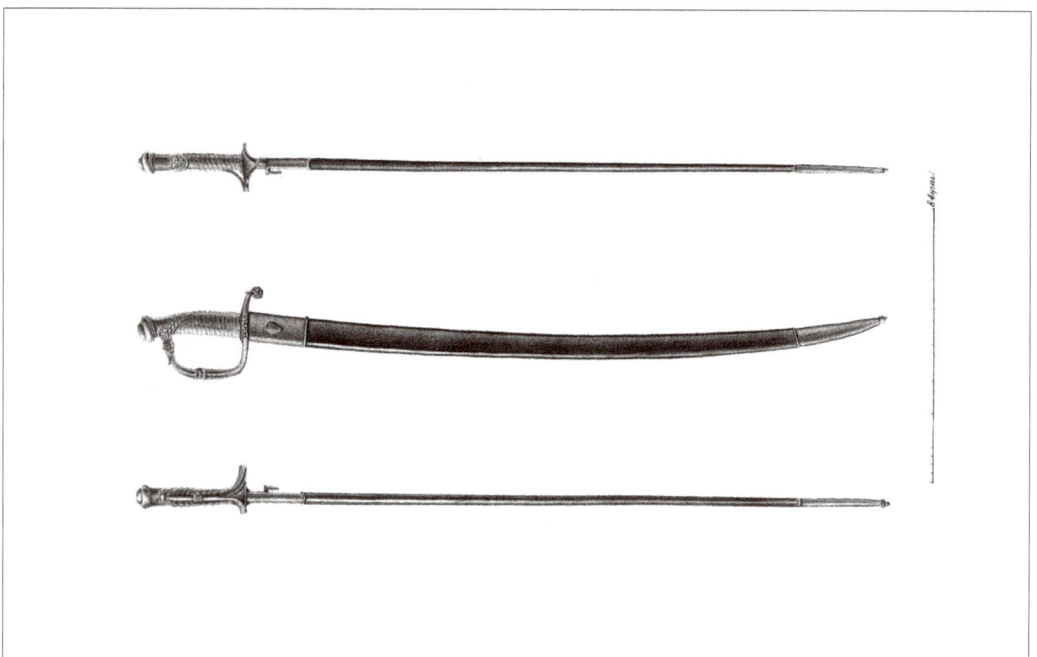

Waistbelt with Frog for Infantry Troops of the Separate Caucasus Corps, confirmed 8 August 1848

Officer's Half-saber with Sword-belt for Infantry Troops of the Separate Caucasus Corps, confirmed 8 August 1848

Infantry Officer's Gold Half-saber " For Courage ", confirmed 24 December 1849

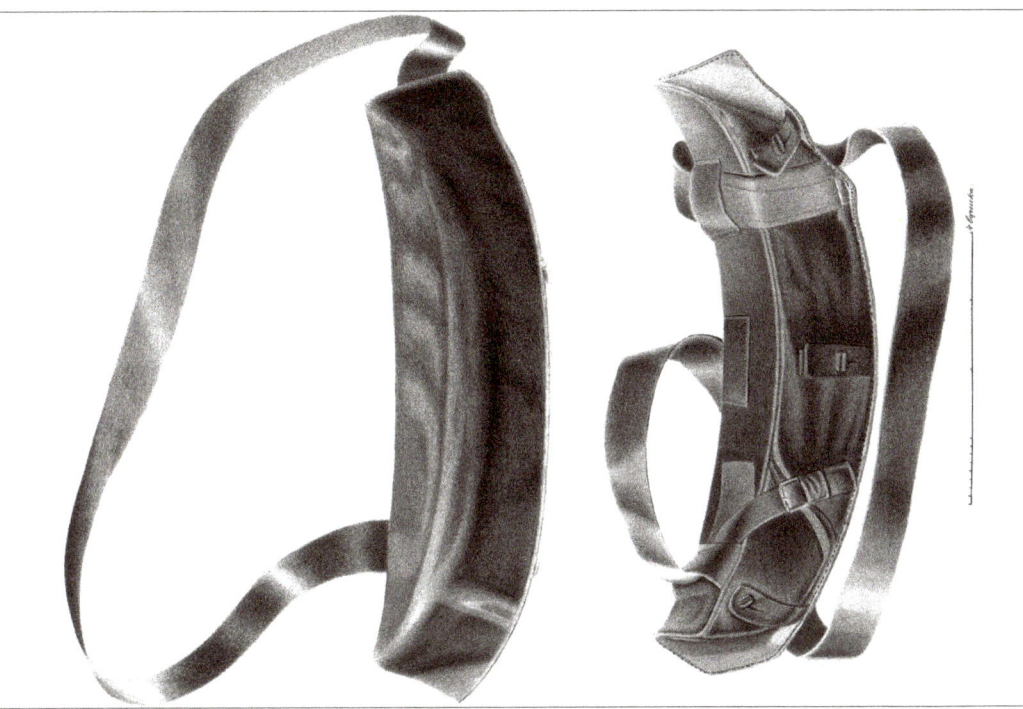

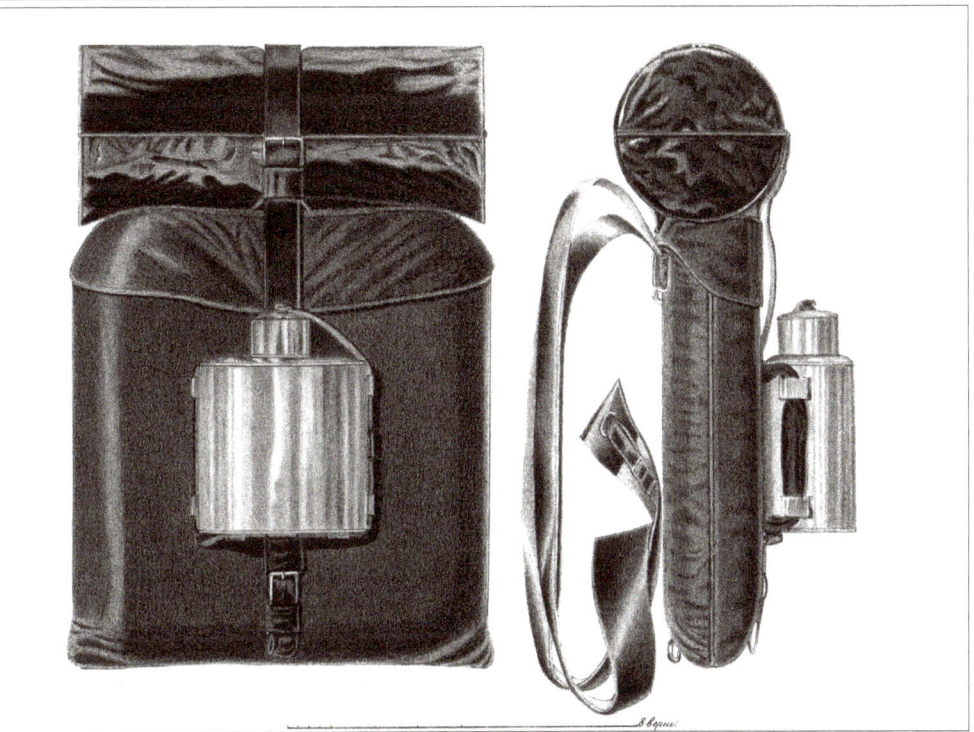

Lower Rank's Ammunition Pouch for Infantry Troops of the Separate Caucasus Corps, confirmed 8 August 1848

Lower Rank's Knapsack for Infantry Troops of the Separate Caucasus Corps, confirmed 8 August 1848

Company-grade Officers. His imperial Grenadier Regiment. 1848-1855

Non-combatant. His imperial Grenadier Regiment. 1848-1855

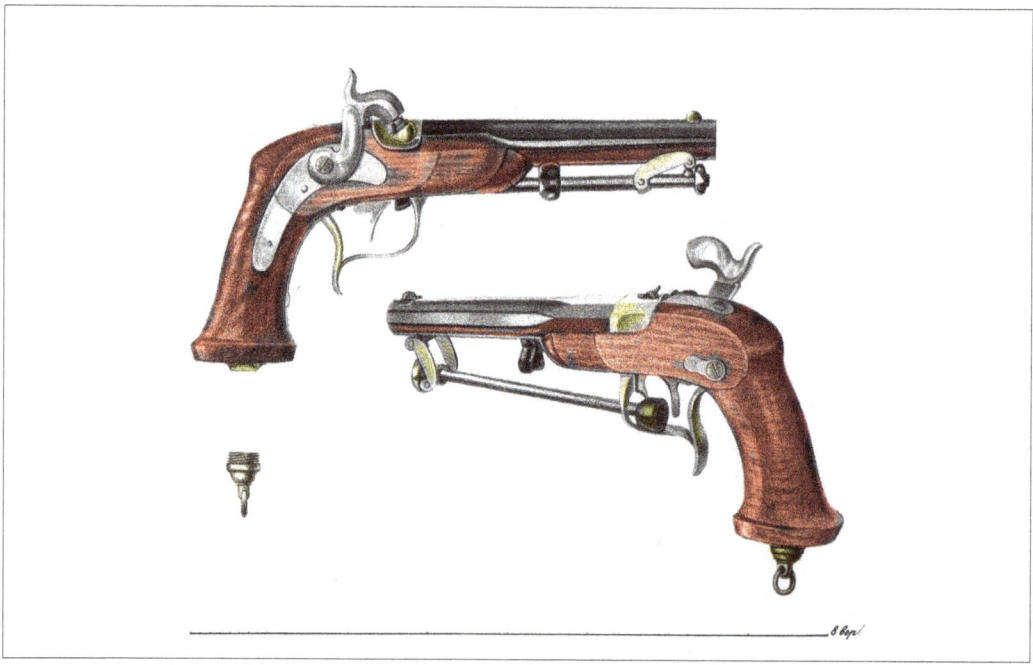

Infantry Signal Bugle (English Pattern), confirmed 19 April 1849

Infantry Officer's Percussion Pistol, confirmed 14 September 1849

Bugler. Grenadier Regiments. 1849-1855.

Lower Rank's Helmet for Grenadier Regiments, confirmed 9 and 25 November 1849

Non-commissioned Officer. Grenadier Regiments. 1851-1855

Private. Grenadier Regiments. 1851-1854

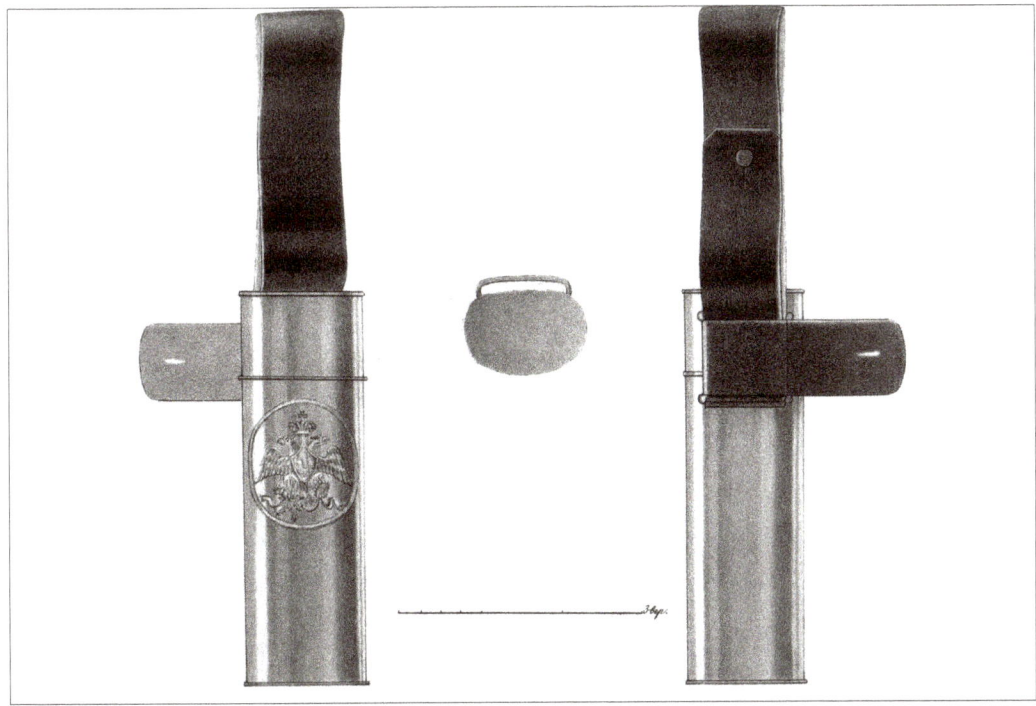

Infantry Drum, confirmed 8 July 1851 - Fife Case for Infantry Troops of the Separate Caucasus Corps, confirmed 8 July 1851

Fifer. His imperial Grenadier Regiment. 1851-1855

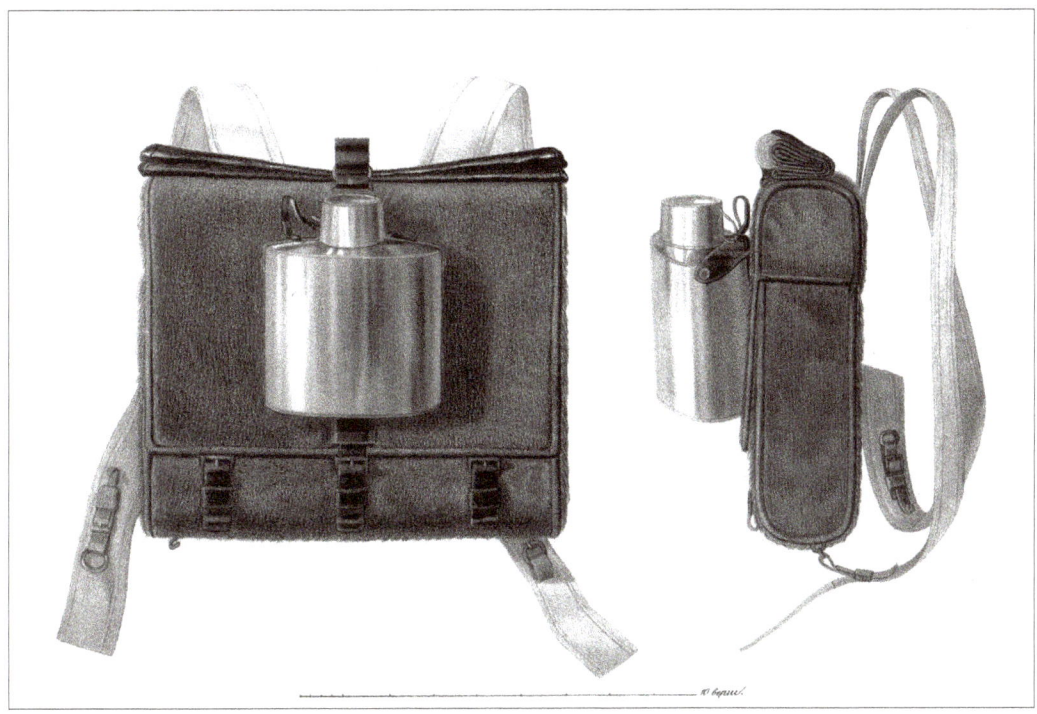

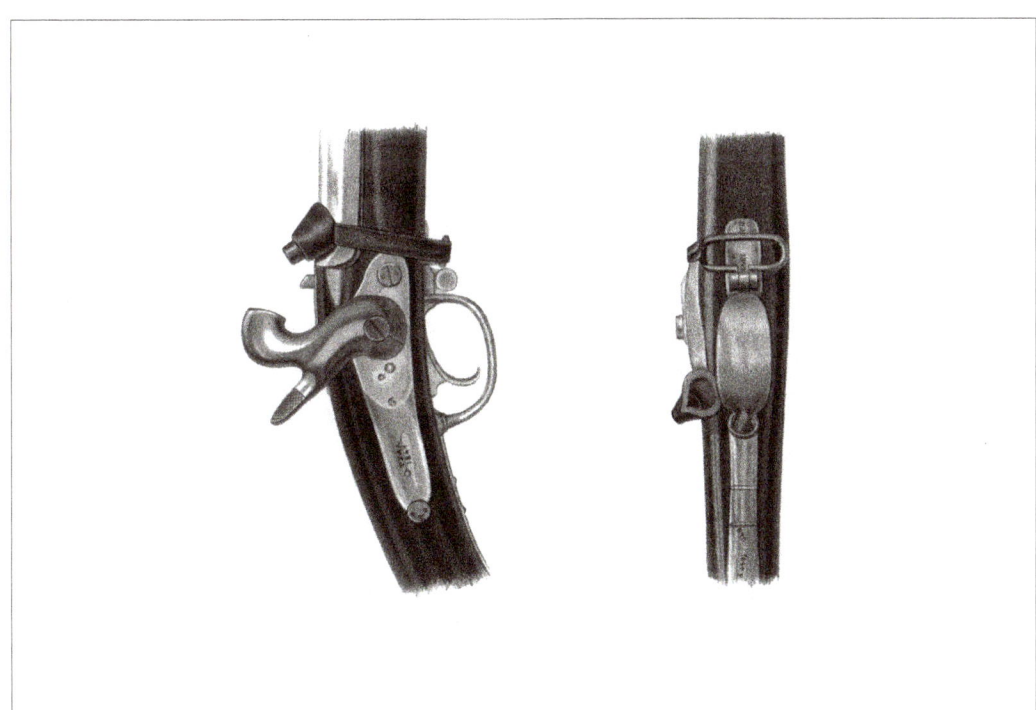

Infantry Water Flask and Greatcoat Strap, confirmed July 8th 1851 - Firing-Nipple Cover for Percussion Infantry Muskets, confirmed 8 July 1851

Non-combatant. Grenadier Regiments. 1852-1855

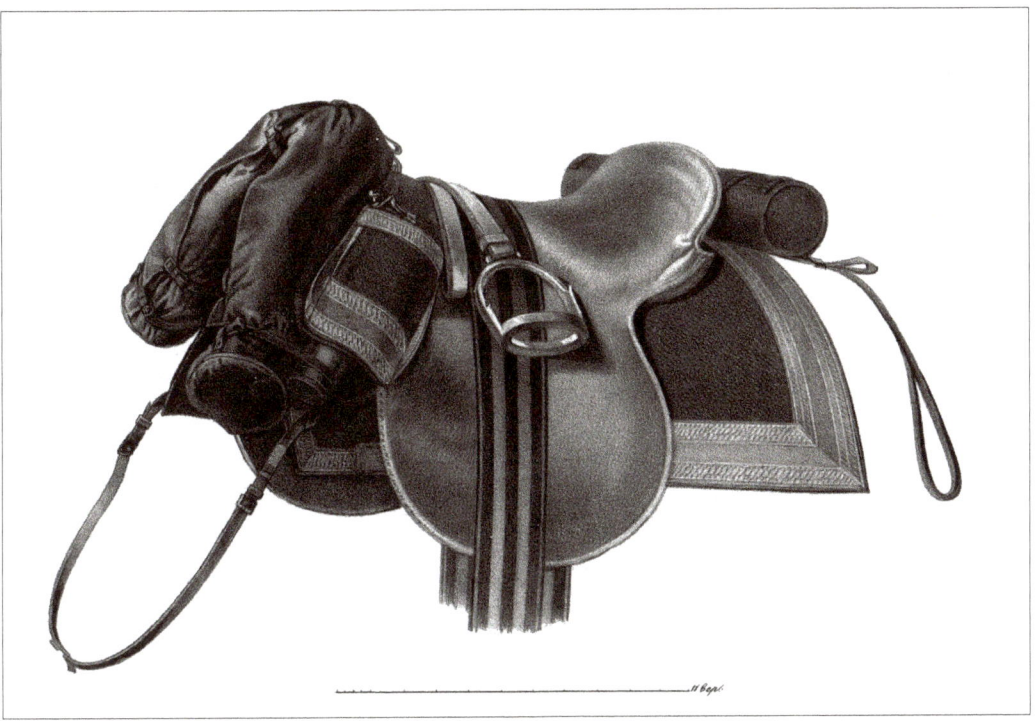

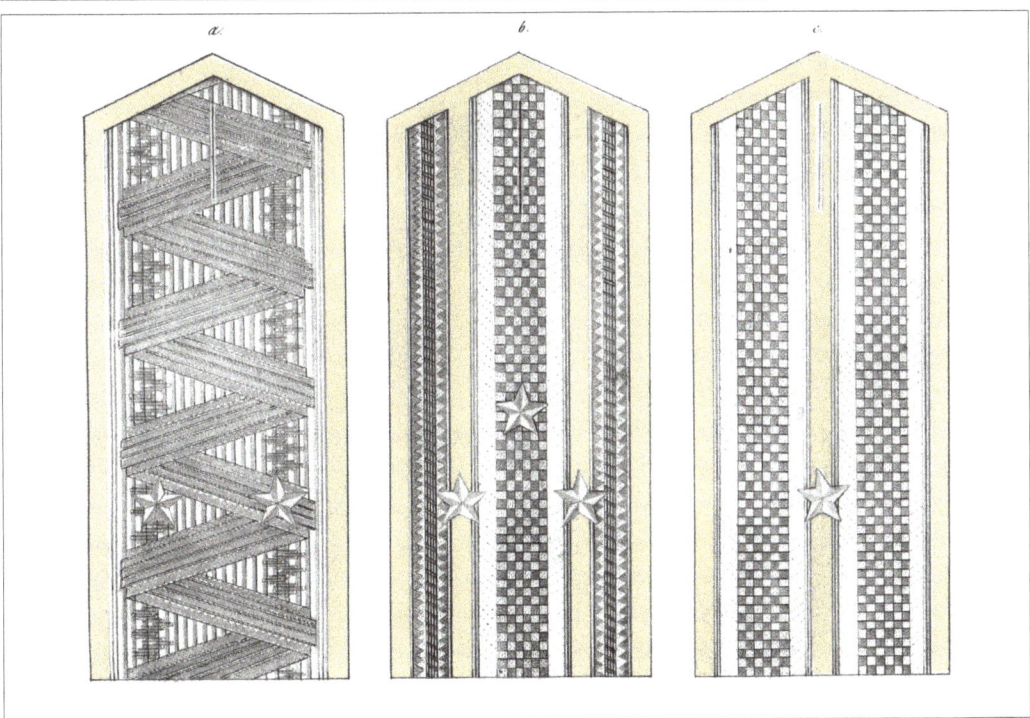

Infantry Officer's Horse Furniture, confirmed 18 February 1854 - Campaign Greatcoat Shoulder Straps for Grenadier Regiments, established April 29th 1854. a) General, b) Field-grade Officer, and c) Company-grade Officer.

Field-grade Officer. Grenadier Regiments. 1854 and 1855

Company-grade Officer. Grenadier Regiments. 1854 and 1855

Company-grade Officer. Grenadier Regiments. 1854 and 1855

Private. Grenadier Regiments. 1855

Non-commissioned Officers. Musketeer Companies of Infantry and Marine Regiments. 1826-1828

Drummer. Musketeer Companies of Infantry Regiments. 1826-1828

Company-grade Officers. Infantry Regiments of the Lithuania Corps. 1826-1828

Field-grade Officer and Adjutant. Infantry and Marine Regiments. 1826-1828

Private. Infantry Regiment. 1828-1830

Company-grade Officer. Grenadier Companies of Infantry Regiments. 1826-1833

Shako Plate for Infantry Regiments, confirmed 24 April 1828

Company-grade Officer. Infantry Regiments of the Caucasus Corps. 1830-1834

Shako Badge for Distinction with the Inscription: " For Warsaw 25 and 26 August of the year 1831", confirmed December 6th 1831.

Officer's Epaulette and Lower Rank's Shoulder Strap for The Prince of Prussia's Infantry Regiment, confirmed 25 July 1840

Company-grade Officer and Non-commissioned Officer. Infantry Regiments. 1833-1835

Company-grade Officer and Private. Marine Regiments. 1833-1846

Shako Plate for Infantry Regiments, confirmed 5 May 1833

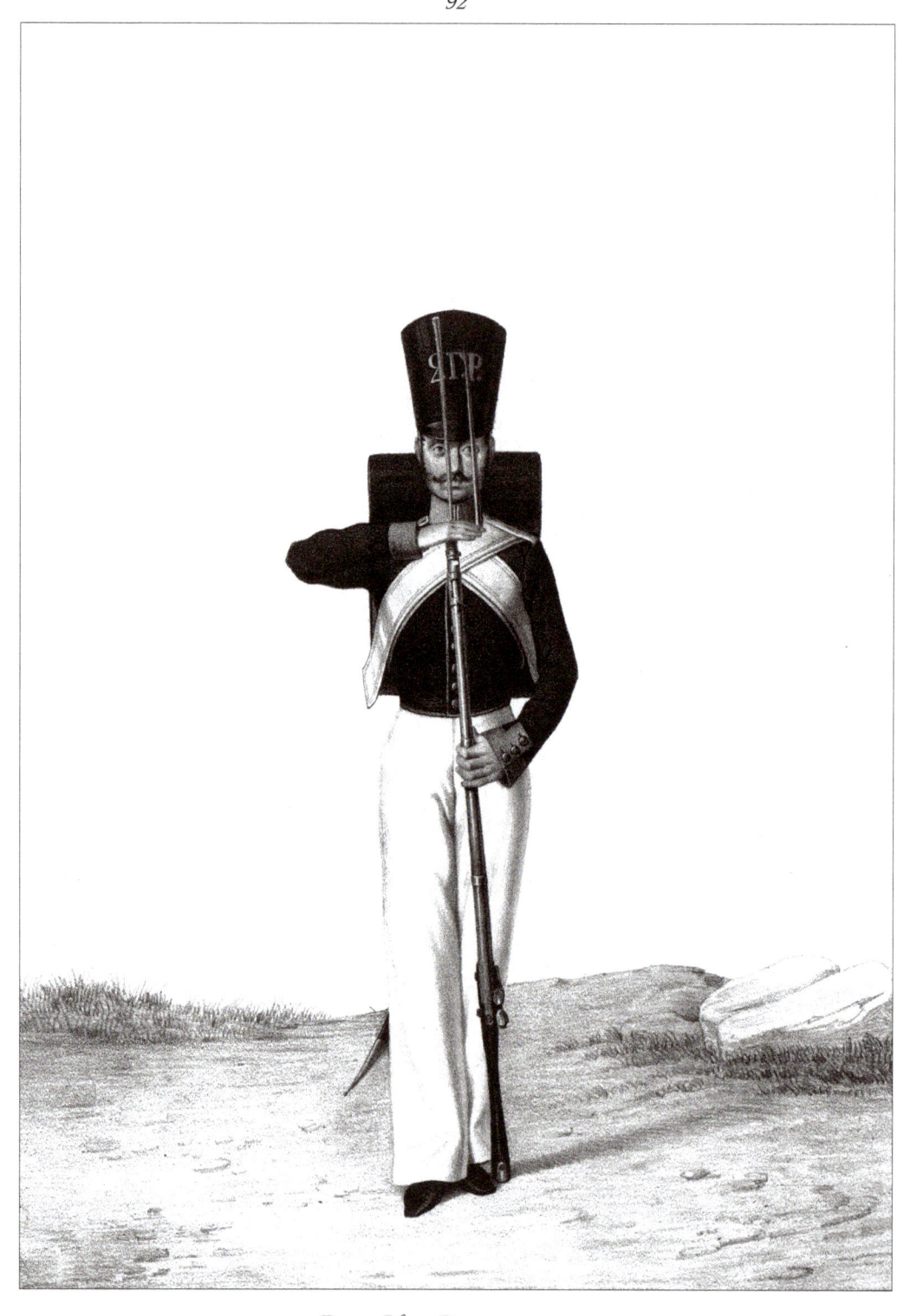

Private. Infantry Regiments. 1835-1843

Company-grade Officer. Musketeer Companies of Infantry Regiments. 1835-1843

Grenadier. Infantry Regiments. 1843 and 1844

Non-commissioned Officer and Company-grade Officer. Infantry Regiments. 1844-1846

Field-grade Officer. Infantry Regiments. 1845-1849

Field-grade Officer. His Majesty the King of Naples' Infantry Regiment. 1846-1849

Officer's Epaulette and Lower Rank's Shoulder Strap of His Majesty the King of Naples' Infantry Regiment, confirmed 21 January 1846

Officer's Epaulette and Lower Rank's Shoulder Strap of His Majesty the King of Sardinia's Infantry Regiment, confirmed 1 February 1846

Company-grade Officer. His Majesty the King of Sardinia's Infantry Regiment. 1846-1848. Note: In 1848 this regiment became His Imperial Highness the Grand Duke Vladimir Aleksandrovich's Infantry Regiment

Private. His Majesty the King of Naples' Infantry Regiment. 1846-1849

Privates. Infantry Regiments of the Separate Caucasus Corps. 1848-1855

Field-grade Officer. Infantry Regiments of the Separate Caucasus Corps. 1848-1855

Drummer. Infantry Regiments. 1851-1855

SOLDIERS, WEAPONS & UNIFORMS ALREADY PUBLISHED
(SOME TITLES)

UNIFORMS OF RUSSIAN ARMY IN THE ERA OF ANCIENT TZAR
FROM THE REIGN OF VASILI IV TO MICHAEL I, ALEXIS, FEODOR III DURING THE XVII th CENTURY
A.V.VISKOVATOV — LUCA STEFANO CRISTINI
SWU-600-004

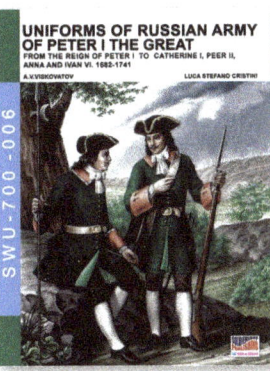

UNIFORMS OF RUSSIAN ARMY OF PETER I THE GREAT
FROM THE REIGN OF PETER I TO CATHERINE I, PEER II, ANNA AND IVAN VI. 1682-1741
A.V.VISKOVATOV — LUCA STEFANO CRISTINI
SWU-700-006

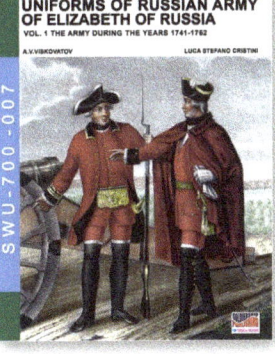

UNIFORMS OF RUSSIAN ARMY OF ELIZABETH OF RUSSIA
VOL. 1 THE ARMY DURING THE YEARS 1741-1762
A.V.VISKOVATOV — LUCA STEFANO CRISTINI
SWU-700-007

UNIFORMS OF RUSSIAN ARMY OF ELIZABETH OF RUSSIA
VOL. 2 THE ARMY DURING THE YEARS 1741-1762
A.V.VISKOVATOV — LUCA STEFANO CRISTINI
SWU-700-008

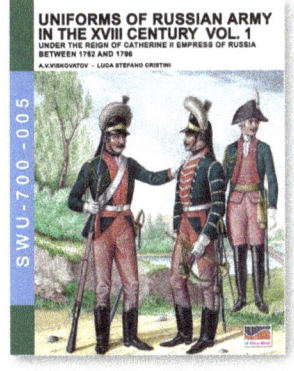

UNIFORMS OF RUSSIAN ARMY IN THE XVIII CENTURY VOL. 1
UNDER THE REIGN OF CATHERINE II EMPRESS OF RUSSIA BETWEEN 1762 AND 1796
A.V.VISKOVATOV — LUCA STEFANO CRISTINI
SWU-700-005

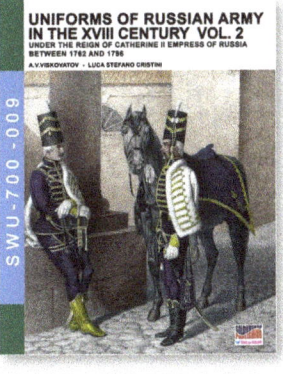

UNIFORMS OF RUSSIAN ARMY IN THE XVIII CENTURY VOL. 2
UNDER THE REIGN OF CATHERINE II EMPRESS OF RUSSIA BETWEEN 1762 AND 1796
A.V.VISKOVATOV — LUCA STEFANO CRISTINI
SWU-700-009

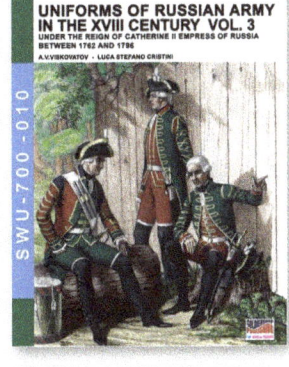

UNIFORMS OF RUSSIAN ARMY IN THE XVIII CENTURY VOL. 3
UNDER THE REIGN OF CATHERINE II EMPRESS OF RUSSIA BETWEEN 1762 AND 1796
A.V.VISKOVATOV — LUCA STEFANO CRISTINI
SWU-700-010

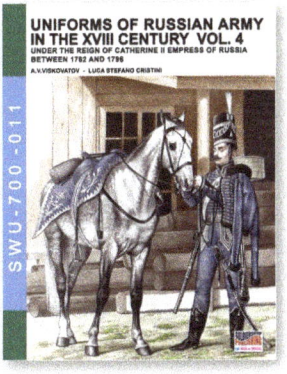

UNIFORMS OF RUSSIAN ARMY IN THE XVIII CENTURY VOL. 4
UNDER THE REIGN OF CATHERINE II EMPRESS OF RUSSIA BETWEEN 1762 AND 1796
A.V.VISKOVATOV — LUCA STEFANO CRISTINI
SWU-700-011

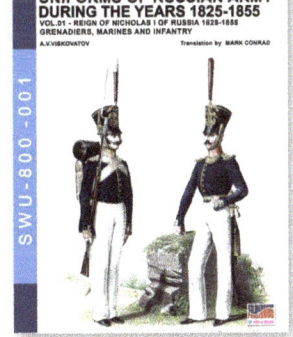

UNIFORMS OF RUSSIAN ARMY DURING THE YEARS 1825-1855
VOL.01 - REIGN OF NICHOLAS I OF RUSSIA 1825-1855 GRENADIERS, MARINES AND INFANTRY
A.V.VISKOVATOV   Translation by MARK CONRAD
SWU-800-001

UNIFORMS OF RUSSIAN ARMY DURING THE YEARS 1825-1855
VOL.02 - REIGN OF NICHOLAS I OF RUSSIA 1825-1855 CARABINIERS, JÄGERS, RIFLES, AND CUIRASSIERS
A.V.VISKOVATOV   Translation by MARK CONRAD
SWU-800-002

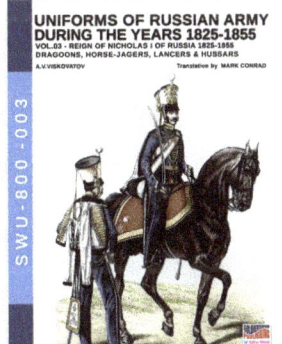

UNIFORMS OF RUSSIAN ARMY DURING THE YEARS 1825-1855
VOL.03 - REIGN OF NICHOLAS I OF RUSSIA 1825-1855 DRAGOONS, HORSE-JAGERS, LANCERS & HUSSARS
A.V.VISKOVATOV   Translation by MARK CONRAD
SWU-800-003

UNIFORMS OF RUSSIAN ARMY DURING THE YEARS 1825-1855
VOL.04 - REIGN OF NICHOLAS I OF RUSSIA 1825-1855 GENDARMES, TRAIN, ARTILLERY, SAPPERS & PIONEERS
A.V.VISKOVATOV   Translation by MARK CONRAD
SWU-800-004

UNIFORMS OF RUSSIAN ARMY DURING THE NAPOLEONIC WAR
VOL.9 - REIGN OF PAUL I 1796 AND 1801 - THE GUARDS 1
A.V.VISKOVATOV   TRANSLATION BY MARK CONRAD
EBOOK SWU-NAP-010

UNIFORMS OF RUSSIAN ARMY DURING THE NAPOLEONIC WAR
VOL.10 - REIGN OF ALEXANDER I OF RUSSIA 1801-1825 CAVALRY: CUIRASSIERS, DRAGOONS & HORSE-JÄGERS
A.V.VISKOVATOV   Translation by MARK CONRAD
SWU-NAP-015

UNIFORMS OF RUSSIAN ARMY DURING THE NAPOLEONIC WAR
VOL.11 - REIGN OF ALEXANDER I OF RUSSIA 1801-1825 CAVALRY: HUSSARS, LANCERS, GENDARMES, & THE TRAIN
A.V.VISKOVATOV   Translation by MARK CONRAD
SWU-NAP-016

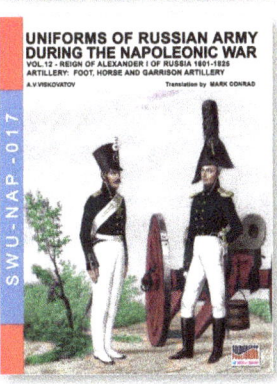

UNIFORMS OF RUSSIAN ARMY DURING THE NAPOLEONIC WAR
VOL.12 - REIGN OF ALEXANDER I OF RUSSIA 1801-1825 ARTILLERY: FOOT, HORSE AND GARRISON ARTILLERY
A.V.VISKOVATOV   Translation by MARK CONRAD
SWU-NAP-017